Reading Their Way

A Balance of Phonics and Whole Language

Dor

D0878991

A SCARECROWEDUCATION BOOK

The Scarecrow Press, Inc.
Lanham, Maryland, and Oxford
2003

A SCARECROWEDUCATION BOOK

Published in the United States of America
by Scarecrow Press, Inc.
A Member of the Rowman & Littlefield Publishing Group
4720 Boston Way, Lanham, Maryland 20706
www.scarecroweducation.com

PO Box 317
Oxford
OX2 9RU, UK

British Library Cataloguing in Publication Information Available

Library of Congress Cataloging-in-Publication Data
Donat, Dorothy J., 1953–
    Reading their way : a balance of phonics and whole language / Dorothy
J. Donat.
        p. cm.
"A ScarecrowEducation book."
Includes bibliographical references.
    ISBN 0-8108-4548-2 (hard : alk. paper) — ISBN 0-8108-4549-0 (pbk. :
alk. paper)
    1. Reading (Early childhood)   I. Title.
    LB1139.5.R43 D66 2003
    372.4—dc21   2002010565

♾ᵀᴹ The paper used in this publication meets the minimum requirements of
American National Standard for Information Sciences—Permanence of
Paper for Printed Library Materials, ANSI/NISO Z39.48-1992.
Manufactured in the United States of America.

To Dennis, Adam and Holly for their patience and encouragement while I was writing this book.

To all of the children I've taught because they were such great teachers for me.

Contents

Chapter One

An Overview:

Why *Reading Their Way?*

"Teacher, I know you're busy; but sometime today I hope you will teach me how to read." Oh, the innocent exclamation of a kindergarten child on the first day of school. Oh, the motivation of a kindergarten child on the first day of school. Oh, the challenge for the teacher!

What is the best way to answer this challenge? Teachers every day, everywhere are confronted with this question. With the guidance of the *Reading Their Way* approach, teachers, children and parents have turned this challenge into a great opportunity.

Reading Their Way is a balanced approach to literacy beginning in kindergarten and extending through third grade. It is built around four components that are research based and proven to be effective. These components include: phonological awareness, phonics, contextual reading, and writing. Each of these areas will be discussed in the chapters to follow. "To be successful in teaching all children to read and write, we have to do it all!" (Cunningham, Hall and Sigmon, *The Teacher's Guide to the Four Blocks*, 1999.) With the balance of the *Reading Their Way* approach, we can do it all.

Reading Their Way was initiated in the Augusta County school division of Virginia. The kindergarten portion is an adaptation of unpublished work by Betty Grissom, Director, Discovery Montessori School, Jacksonville Beach, Florida. Grissom designed a systematic method to introduce beginning reading skills to children in preschool or kindergarten. *Reading Their Way* has adapted and extended that model while adding sound sequences and guidance for kindergarten through third grade (see appendix A).

Reading Their Way has been implemented around a time schedule that incorporates parallel block scheduling as developed by Robert Lynn Canady. This scheduling strategy is highly recommended. It increases opportunities for small group instruction, remediation and enrichment. This time schedule also allows multiple, face-to-face interactions between the teacher and the child. Combining the *Reading Their Way* curriculum with the parallel block time schedule has proven to be very effective.

Initially, the two schools with the greatest need were selected as the pilot sites for this approach to reading instruction. Their need was determined by the percentage of children receiving free or reduced-price lunch. Test scores also were utilized to determine the schools in greatest need. Local and state test results were analyzed.

The children in this school division are faced with state-mandated testing beginning in third grade. These are high-stakes tests that determine school accreditation and, eventually, graduation for the students. All of the tests are written, thus requiring reading on the part of the student. In an effort to increase achievement in reading and to help students be successful on assessments, the goal was set to increase the number of students reading on the third-grade level when they enter third grade. *Reading Their Way* was implemented to meet this goal.

This goal is also important because of the content requirements of the curriculum. In most school divisions, by third grade the emphasis has changed from "learning to read" to "reading to learn." It is imperative that students read on grade level in order to comprehend more easily the content material. *Reading Their Way* can meet this goal.

Data have been collected to determine the effectiveness of *Reading Their Way*. One instrument of data collection is the PALS assessment, developed at the University of Virginia. This is a screening of literacy skills possessed by children at the kindergarten through third-grade levels. Results of the PALS (Phonological Awareness Literacy Screening) help to determine the reading level of the students as well as which literacy skills are in need of strengthening. Figures 1.1 and 1.2 show those results over a period of three years, at the kindergarten level.

Data also are collected from informal reading inventories. Table 1.1 indicates results of *Reading Their Way* versus non-*Reading Their Way* sites. When implementing this approach in kindergarten, students progressed a full year beyond what was normally achieved. Kindergarten

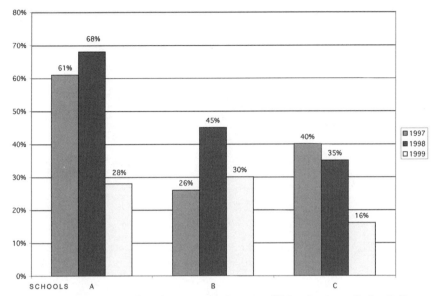

Figure 1.1. Percentage of Kindergarten Students Qualifying for Remediation/Fall

Note: This graph depicts data from the PALS test, which is given to kindergarten students in October. The graph shows a three-year comparison for three schools. These data reflect the percentage of students who did not meet the benchmark and thus required remedial instruction. Schools A and C had begun "Reading Their Way" at the beginning of the 1999 school year and had significantly fewer students requiring remediation. School B had not begun "Reading Their Way" and the data show a relatively high percentage of students requiring remediation. All of these schools are Title I schools, with B being the least needy by eligibility standards.

Source: Phonological Awareness Literacy Screening, University of Virginia (Fall, 1997, 1998, 1999)

children began to read approximately six weeks into the school year. Previously, the majority of students did not begin reading until first or second grade.

Below are listed many facets of *Reading Their Way* that have proven to be highlights of this approach for guiding children through their literacy development. Each of these highlights will be discussed further in the following chapters. *Reading Their Way*

- Includes multiple phonological and phonemic awareness activities
- Teaches with manipulatives rather than workbooks
- Focuses on letter sounds rather than letter names
- Focuses on lower case letters rather than upper case letters
- Introduces vowels earlier and blending using word families

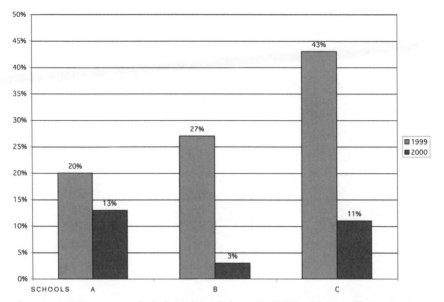

Figure 1.2.   Percentage of Kindergarten Students Qualifying for Remediation/Spring

Note: This graph depicts data from the PALS test, which was given in May. The graph shows a two-year comparison for three schools. These data reflect the percentage of students who did not meet the benchmark and thus continue to require remediation. School A shows improvement, while Schools B and C show significant improvement over last year's spring scores.

Source: Phonological Awareness Literacy Screening, University of Virginia (Spring, 1999, 2000)

- Begins reading of books as soon as child starts to blend sounds into words
- Incorporates comprehension strategies
- Includes some form of writing every day

Why *Reading Their Way*? Because it works! It is academic while respecting the developmental stages through which children progress. The students are very proud of their accomplishments. Parents are amazed that their children begin to read so quickly and sustain that progress. Teachers feel very successful. Research by Marilyn Jager Adams (1990) indicates that the approaches in which systematic code instruction is included along with meaning emphasis, language instruction and connected reading are found to result in superior reading achievement overall. These conclu-´ sions seem at least as valid for children with low reading-readiness profiles as they are for their better prepared and more advantaged peers. Re-

Table 1.1. Percentage of Kindergarten Children Reading at These Levels

School	PrePrimer	Primer	1st Grade
A	12%	0%	0%
B	0%	0%	0%
C	0%	0%	0%
D	7%	1%	1%
*E	60%	0%	20%
F	0%	0%	0%
G	0%	0%	0%
*H	35%	4%	5%
I	0%	0%	0%
J	13%	3%	0%
*K	27%	2%	3%
L	0%	2%	0%

* Sites utilizing *Reading Their Way*

Note: This table depicts the reading level of students as they finished kindergarten in spring, 2000. The data indicate the percentage of students reading at that level. Schools E, H, and K had implemented the "Reading Their Way" approach and are the same schools as referenced respectively as A, B, C in figure 1.1 and figure 1.2.

Source: Word Recognition in Isolation Assessment, PALS, University of Virginia (Spring, 2000)

sults of G. Reid Lyon's research in "Why Johnny Can't Decode" (1996) stress the importance of an instructional program composed of direct instruction in phonological awareness, phonics and contextual reading skills. *Reading Their Way* endorses the Adams and Lyon research with the addition of the writing component to fulfill the balance.

Have a happy journey through this book. Enjoy learning how to increase student achievement and develop lifelong learners. You will make a difference!

Chapter Two

The Phonological
Awareness Component

When you listen to someone speak, do you listen for every syllable in every word? I doubt it. *Gen-er-al-ly speak-ing, we do not lis-ten for each syl-la-ble. Ra-ther, we are try-ing to dis-cern the mean-ing of what the per-son is say-ing.* Children are like this as well. They are trying to make sense of the spoken message. They are not attending to each and every syllable.

However, this understanding that speech is made up of segments is very important. Indeed words do have syllables. Words do have a beginning, middle and ending. Children need to be able to hear all of those different segments in order to learn to read and write. We refer to this understanding as phonological awareness.

More discriminately, words are composed of individual sounds. These small units of sound are called phonemes. Children need to develop the awareness of the individual sounds; we refer to this as phonemic awareness. This understanding is necessary as they learn to decode words while reading and encode words while writing. Phonological awareness and phonemic awareness are basic to learning to read and are a strong component of the *Reading Their Way* approach. These are auditory processes and do not involve the relationship between letter sound and the printed alphabetic symbol. That relationship is phonics.

Phonological and phonemic awareness do not come naturally to many children. When they listen to someone speak, the children are focusing on understanding the message. Children are not necessarily thinking about the words themselves, much less syllables, individual sounds, etc. However, the good news is that this awareness can be taught. Studies conducted by Lundberg et al. (1988), show that children who receive specific training in phonological awareness are able to learn to read more quickly than children of similar backgrounds who did not receive such training.

Children progress through stages of development as they grow in their phonological and phonemic awareness. These stages vary in level of difficulty. Stated below are the levels from the easiest to the most demanding:

Listening Skills
Rhyming Skills
Understanding Syllables
Blending Phonemes
Segmenting Phonemes
Manipulating Phonemes

One of the first phonological awareness skills teachers should emphasize is listening. This is the easiest skill but very basic to the development of higher-level skills. Kindergarten teachers should begin working on listening activities on the first day of school. Such activities are listed at the end of this chapter.

Rhyming is another skill that is usually one of the first taught by kindergarten teachers. Children need to be able to discriminate words that rhyme from those that do not. Nursery rhymes are a great way to instruct this skill. Hearing rhyme involves hearing segments of sound and thus phonological and phonemic awareness are emphasized.

As understandings progress, children will be able to produce rhyming words. They will be able to develop a list of rhyming words if the teacher provides the exemplar. This is a higher level of understanding than recognizing rhyme when the teacher provides the words.

As stated earlier, phonological and phonemic awareness are auditory in nature. However, connections need to be made between speech and print. Therefore, a child's attention should be drawn to print in conjunction with the presentation of auditory activities.

Children need to be aware that their speech matches print. They need to be encouraged to point to words as they recite nursery rhymes, poems, songs on charts, etc. Activities need to be provided where the child counts the number of words in a sentence. Children need to track the printed words as they recite the text. This will develop their concept of word. Teacher and student dialog contrasting a letter from a word is very important. Teacher and student dialog contrasting a word from a sentence is very important. All of this in conjunction with phonological awareness activities leads to a balance that is so important.

As children are thinking about "word," they also can concentrate on the segments of words in the form of syllables. This is the next level of instruction for the development of phonological awareness skills. Again, this is auditory in nature. Teachers utilize strategies and activities that encourage children to discriminate and segment words by syllables. This understanding generally develops before the fine tuning of phonemic awareness. Activities to encourage the identification of syllables are listed at the end of this chapter.

Instruction at this point turns from the more general phonological awareness to the more definitive phonemic awareness. Children are asked to identify and utilize individual sounds or phonemes. Instruction involves blending of sounds. Teachers begin with a focus upon the beginning sound and blending it with the rest of the word. This is referred to as the blending of the onset (initial sound) and rime (vowel and everything that follows). Sorting pictures by beginning sounds will become very important at this time. Again, these are auditory skills. The issue is whether the child can "hear" the beginning sounds of words. It is not necessary, at this point, that the children identify the letter that makes that sound. The issue is only that the sound can be identified. As understanding develops, teachers will emphasize the middle and ending sounds of words.

The next level of phonemic awareness involves segmenting phonemes. Can the child state that /man/ is segmented as /m/ /a/ /n/? Usually this understanding develops initially from the segmentation of the beginning sound, segmenting the onset from the rime. Then segmentation progresses to the ending sound and lastly the medial sound.

Once children are able to segment phonemes they are ready for instruction involving manipulating those phonemes. They should be instructed with strategies and activities where the phonemes are changed to make new words. For instance, if the /m/ in /mat/ is changed to /p/, the word becomes /pat/. Likewise, if the /t/ in /mat/ is changed to /n/, the word becomes /man/. Understandings of this nature usually develop from successful manipulation of beginning sound, then ending sound, and lastly the medial sound. Activities to encourage this level of understanding are listed at the end of this chapter.

As Blachman states in *Getting Ready to Read* (1991), teachers need to provide for individual differences in the phonological abilities that are required for reading in an alphabetic system. Teachers need to make sure that all children learn about the segmental nature of speech and how print maps to speech. Instruction needs to incorporate oral language games, rhyming, repeated opportunities to connect printed and spoken words when being read to, and by opportunities to write.

Phonological awareness and phonemic awareness are basic to learning to read and write. *Reading Their Way* places strong emphasis on the skills to develop this awareness. These are auditory processes. No connection has necessarily been made to the printed symbol just yet. Children can be very successful with phonological tasks even without knowing the names of any letters of the alphabet. Matching sound to alphabetic symbol is phonics. That will be discussed in chapter three.

Phonological awareness and phonemic awareness are so important that they need to be incorporated into a teacher's schedule every day. Such activities need to occur several times each day. Review! Review! Review! This does not bore young children—it builds confidence. Cunningham's study of a kindergarten sample (1990) indicates that post-test reading scores were higher for children who received phonological training than for a comparison group that instead listened to stories and discussed them.

Phonological and phonemic awareness activities are great fun to implement. It is like playing with words. Our language can be very entertaining. Teachers should incorporate such activities when working with their whole class, small groups, or individuals. Slip these skills in whenever possible, even when lining up for lunch, for example.

The following are a few activities that have been implemented successfully in classrooms. Since phonological awareness is usually developed by second grade, the activities listed here are geared to kindergarten–second grade; however, if you have a third-grade student who is a nonreader, assessing his or her phonological skills would be advised. These activities would be beneficial if the assessment indicates a lack of skill development. Consult appendix B for other resources of phonemic awareness activities.

As Juel (1988) found when she followed the reading development of fifty-four children from first to fourth grade, the poorest readers at the end of fourth grade were the ones who began first grade with little phonemic awareness. As a result, they did not develop good decoding skills in first grade. Without good word recognition skills, Juel found that these children were the ones who disliked reading and did less of it, losing valuable opportunities for vocabulary growth and for exposure to new concepts and ideas.

SUGGESTED ACTIVITIES TO DEVELOP PHONOLOGICAL AWARENESS AND PHONEMIC AWARENESS

Audience: Kindergarten–Second Grade
Time Commitment: 25 percent of the reading/language arts block of time

LISTENING

1. Name That Sound: Play a tape of familiar sounds and see if the children can identify those sounds (e.g. dog barking, fire engine siren, doorbell, pencil sharpener). It is also fun to tape voices of classmates and encourage other classmates to try to identify those voices.
2. Nursery Rhyme Mistake: Read a familiar nursery rhyme but change a word and see if the children notice your "mistake" (e.g. Jack and Jill went up the hill to fetch a pot of daisies).
3. Where Are You?: Have one child close his or her eyes and another child move to a different part of the classroom. The child who moved makes a noise (animal sound or ring a bell) and the child with eyes closed has to tell where the other child is located.
4. Can You Remember?: Give directions for children to follow. Begin with simple one- or two-step directions and then advance to more complicated directions.
5. Copy Cat: The teacher says a sentence and the child must repeat that sentence. Gradually offer more complicated sentences for the child to repeat.

RHYMING

1. Supply the Rhyme: When reading poetry, songs, or jingles, exaggerate the meter and rhyme and encourage the child to actively listen and participate in the reading. As children become more familiar with the text, the teacher should stop before the rhyming word and have the children supply the word.
2. Picture Rhyme: Say words to the child and ask if they rhyme. Next place pictures in a pocket chart and have children match the pictures

that rhyme. Have some pictures that do not rhyme so that children can see the difference. Extend by playing rhyming concentration.

3. Crazy Pot Rhyme: Say four words and have three of them rhyme. Have the child tell which word did not rhyme.
4. Beanbag Rhyme: Have the children stand in a circle. The teacher begins by saying a word. Then the teacher throws a beanbag to a child. That child should give a word that rhymes with the teacher's word. Next, the beanbag is thrown to another classmate and so on. See which rhyming pattern gets the most words. Extend by going on a rhyme hunt in the classroom (e.g. "What rhymes with label?" [table], "What rhymes with hair?" [chair]).
5. Yes-or-No Game: Say two words to the children. If they rhyme, the children connect two cubes, i.e. unifix cubes, of the same color. If the words do not rhyme, the children connect two unifix cubes of different colors. This game would also work by having the child give a "thumbs up" or "thumbs down," depending upon whether the words rhyme or not. They also like to give a smiling face for rhyming words or a frowning face when words do not rhyme.

SYLLABLES

1. Clap-A-Name: Clapping for each syllable in a name is one of the most popular games. This easily could be done as the children are lining up for lunch.
2. Hidden Objects: Place some objects in a bag, making sure that some of them have names that contain multiple syllables. Have a child select an object and the class counts the syllables by clapping. The original child gets to say how many syllables are in the name of the object.
3. Syllable Links: Link connectable cubes, i.e. unifix cubes, to show how many syllables are in a word.
4. Circle Nursery Rhymes: Have the children sit in a circle. Select a child to start and progress around the circle having each child stand for the next syllable as the nursery rhyme is recited. If the rhyme goes "full circle," then the children sit for each syllable.
5. Puppet Talk: The teacher would use a puppet to stretch words into syllables and see if the child can identify the word (e.g. mo-tor-cy-cle).

BLENDING

1. Magical Names: Children love activities that involve their names. Isolate the beginning sound of the child's name from the rest of the name and see if the children can identify the name (e.g. /J/ - /im/). Extend the activity by segmenting all of the phonemes (e.g. /J/ /i/ /m/) and then ask the child to blend together. Further extend this activity with words other than names.
2. Guess My Word: Give clues such as, "I'm thinking of a word that begins with /s/ and you wash with it" (soap).
3. Musical Onset/Rime: Blend onsets and rimes to the tune of "A Hunting We Will Go": A searching we will go, a searching we will go. We'll find a /h/ and add a /orse/, and then we'll have a /horse/.
4. Pop Up People: Have three children sit in chairs (for three phoneme words). Secretly tell each child a sound that represents beginning, middle and ending sound of a word. Each child says the sound in sequence and the class tries to blend the word.
5. Turtle Reading: Read a story to the class, pretending to have trouble blending some words. Say the sounds slowly and let the class listen, blend, and tell the word.

SEGMENTATION

1. Slinky Segmentation: Have the children stretch a slinky as they segment the sounds of words (e.g. stretch the slinky while slowly saying /t/ /a/ /ble/). Extend by thinking of short slinky words and long slinky words.
2. Phoneme Split: Ask children to segment words by onset and rime (e.g. /r/ /un/), also by isolating the final phoneme (/ru/ /n/), and finally by isolating each phoneme (/r/ /u/ /n/).
3. Animal Phoneme Count: Show pictures of animals to class and have the children count how many phonemes are in the name of each animal. Put pictures in cages labeled with the number of phonemes.
4. Clap and Eat Phonemes: Have children count the phonemes by clapping for each one. It is best to have the children say the phonemes as

they count. Extend this activity by inviting the children to tap rhythm sticks, shake rattles, and so forth. Further extend by counting phonemes with marshmallows, candies, etc., and allow the children to eat them at the end of the lesson.

5. Blind Man's Bluff: Have the children close their eyes and hold up fingers to indicate how many phonemes are in the word that you dictate. When everyone has made a guess, have the children open their eyes to check for accuracy.

MANIPULATION

1. Add a Letter: Talk with the class about the /at/ word family. Blend those sounds to make the word "at." Add a letter to the beginning of "at" and have the children discuss the new word, e.g. mat, fat, cat. Model several examples and then ask the children to think of new words that can be made by adding a letter to the beginning of /at/.
2. Phoneme Deletion: The teacher says "pot" and asks the children to say that same word without the /p/, i.e. /ot/, or without the /t/, i.e. /po/.
3. Rhyming Words: Build rhyming words by simply changing the beginning sounds.
4. Puppet Switch: The teacher will have one puppet say a word and a child has another puppet say that same word but with a different beginning sound, middle sound or ending sound.
5. Name Change: Ask the children to change a friend's name by changing one of the sounds in that person's name.

Chapter Three

The Phonics Component

PHONICS VERSUS WHOLE LANGUAGE

Which is best? The battle still rages. In actuality, we need both. The phonics skills dealing with sound/symbol relationships are helpful to children as they learn to read. The emphasis of quality literature and writing associated with the whole language movement is very important as children learn to read. *Reading Their Way* promotes a balance of phonics and whole language. Instruction from both arenas of thought help children to build their repertoire of strategies.

Phonics refers to the correspondence between letter sounds and their written symbols. Whereas phonological awareness is auditory, phonics is visual. Phonics instruction enhances the connection with print that is so vital as children learn to read and write. Children who understand the segmental nature of speech, and who understand how the phonological segments are represented by the letters of an alphabetic writing system, have been shown repeatedly to be more successful in reading and spelling acquisition than children who lack this awareness (Blachman, 1991).

With the *Reading Their Way* approach, children are taught the sound of the letter before the letter name. The goal of letter-sound instruction is to help the children to acquire the relations between printed letters and speech sounds. The names of the letters are neither; they are labels, and care should be taken to avoid blurring their status as such. When children enter school without prior knowledge of the alphabetic code, there is good reason for concern that distinctions between the names and sounds of letters will be confused if they are taught at the same time (Adams, 1990).

17

When children are beginning to read, it is the sound of the letter that is most important, not the name of the letter. The sound of the letter is what helps the child to decode an unknown word or to encode a word when writing. When you ask a child to spell "hat," the child will begin by saying /h/ /hat/. They begin by saying the sounds of the word. They do not begin by saying the names of letters. "Teaching children to recognize letters produces little reading benefit unless the children were also taught the letters' sounds. Research also shows that training in phonemic awareness produces little reading benefit unless children also are taught the printed letters by which each phoneme is represented" (Adams, 1990, pg. 304).

In the *Reading Their Way* approach, manipulatives are utilized to teach children the correspondence between the symbol and sound. Three-dimensional letters are recommended. This allows the child to turn the symbol in a variety of directions to determine which is correct. Magnetic letters are highly recommended. Teachers have found these to be very inviting to children and quite effective. Children love to manipulate the symbols on magnetic dry-erase boards. (See the end of this chapter for suggested activities.)

Reading Their Way phonics lessons are presented in a direct, explicit manner. The object is to keep the lesson as simple as possible. This simplicity particularly benefits our at-risk students because they often have difficulty processing information. It is quite difficult for some children to remember the name of the letter, its upper case symbol, its lower case symbol, as well as its sound. With *Reading Their Way*, instruction has been simplified to those skills that will be used readily by the children. Programs including systematic instruction on letter-to-sound correspondences lead to higher achievement in both word recognition and spelling, at least in the early grades and especially for slower or economically disadvantaged students (Adams, 1990).

Children are taught with the focus on lower case letters. This is because most of the books that students read are written using lower case letters. Their writing experiences also will involve primarily lower case letters. The ability to recognize lowercase letters is more important for reading text (Adams, 1990).

On occasion, the upper case letters certainly are encountered. These upper case letters are seen in books and on room displays. Students are taught to write their names beginning with a capital letter. They are taught to begin sentences with a capital letter. However, the primary focus of instruction remains on the lower case letter symbol. For example, when both upper case and lower case letters are displayed, the teacher will point to the lower case, attempting to draw the attention there.

The *Reading Their Way* sequences for the presentation of the sounds are designed with specific criteria in mind. Sounds are introduced, two at a time. This forces the child to compare and contrast those symbols and their sounds. Care is taken that the letters being simultaneously introduced are not similar in sound. Care is also taken that the symbols do not visually look similar. This special selection of sounds/symbols allows sorting activities to proceed with little confusion. Sorting activities are a part of word study, which is promoted by the McGuffey Reading Center at the University of Virginia. Word study, one approach to phonics instruction, uses a compare-and-contrast approach to word features. Instructional activities consist of sorting tasks, first with picture cards, and then, as words become known, with word cards (Invernizzi et al., 2000).

INTRODUCTION OF SOUNDS

When sounds are introduced, the lesson is composed of three parts: input, recognition and production.

Input

First, the three-dimensional symbol is displayed and the teacher says, "This is /m/. Can you say /m/? This is /t/. Can you say /t/?" The child responds as prompted. Repeat this step as needed to ensure understanding by the child. This is the input stage of introduction.

Recognition

Second, the teacher displays both letter symbols and asks the child to point to /m/ or /t/. The teacher says the sound of the letters and asks the child to point to them. The child responds as prompted. The teacher switches the letters around and prompts the child with the same directions for pointing to sounds. This is the recognition stage of introduction of sounds. Repeat this step as needed for understanding by the child.

Production

Last, the teacher points to a letter symbol and says, "What is this?" The child responds with the correct sound. The symbols may be switched around several times, followed by the same prompt. Repeat as needed for understanding by the child. This is the production stage of the introduction of sounds.

This method of introduction is used each time new sounds are encountered in the sequence. As sounds are learned, the knowledge will be applied to sorting pictures and words by their beginning sounds. Later, words will be sorted by their medial and ending sounds. If words are being sorted, it is vital that the child be able to read the words. Otherwise, the student will have difficulty relating to the different phonemes and their positions in the words.

Once the first short vowel is learned, children are taught to blend the known sounds into words. This blending is modeled by the teacher and practiced as needed according to the pace of understanding. Children are taught to blend from the beginning phoneme to the medial phoneme and then adding the final sound (e.g. /c/ /a/ /t/ = cat). Once confidence is gained with this procedure, word families are explored as "chunks" (e.g. /c/ /at/ = cat). This increases the speed of blending and allows students to make use of their knowledge of onset and rime. As stated in Snow, Burns and Griffin, *Preventing Reading Difficulties in Young Children* (1998), it is not necessary to wait until a child knows all the letters of the alphabet to start explicit instruction in decoding—knowledge of the sound value of a few consonants and vowels may be enough on which to build phonemic awareness and initial word reading instruction (Fielding-Barnesley, 1997).

Picture sorts, object sorts and word sorts are appropriate for kindergarten through third grade. *Words Their Way* by Bear, Invernizzi, Templeton and Johnston (1996) is a great resource for teachers who wish to increase their knowledge of spelling development and word study. Kathy Ganske's *Word Journeys* (2000) is a wonderful resource of spelling inventories and their instructional implications.

THE KINDERGARTEN SOUND SEQUENCE

The sounds are presented in the following sequence:

/m/ vs /t/

/p/ vs /r/

/s/ vs /a/

/at/ word family

/ap/ word family

/ap/ vs /at/ word families

/am/ word family

/at/ vs /ap/ vs /am/ word families

/c/ vs /n/

/b/ vs /o/

/ot/ word family

/op/ word family

/ot/ vs /op/ word families

/ob/ word family

/ot/ vs /op/ vs /ob/ word families

/l/ vs /f/

/h/ vs /d/

/g/ vs /i/

/it/ word family

/ig/ word family

/it/ vs /ig/ word families

/id/ word family

/it/ vs /ig/ vs /id/ word families

/k/ vs /v/

/j/ vs /u/

/ug/ word family

/ut/ word family

/ug/ vs /ut/ word family

/up/ word family

/ug/ vs /ut/ vs /up/ word families

/z/ vs /y/

/w/ vs /e/

/et/ word family

/eg/ word family

/et/ vs /eg/ word families

/ed/ word family

/et/ vs /eg/ vs /ed/ word families

/qu/ vs /x/

/ch/ vs /th/

/sh/ vs /wh/

In kindergarten, the vowels are taught as short vowel sounds. Long vowels are introduced in kindergarten if instructionally appropriate. Otherwise that level of instruction takes place in first grade and so on. Blends and digraphs are introduced in kindergarten as developmentally appropriate.

Application of skills is very important. Once children have begun making words by blending the sounds, they should be immersed in books that have those phonetically regular spelling patterns. Children can decode these words and read them. The children need many opportunities to read and reread these materials.

As students interact with books, they will encounter words that are not necessarily decodable and thus need to be explicitly taught. Display of these words on the classroom wall is an appropriate method of instruction. Creating multiple opportunities for interaction with this wall display is imperative. Matching these words to text or creating bingo word games are very appropriate. Flash cards are another method of explicit instruction that will help children learn these words. Always follow such instruction of isolated words with reading in connected text.

These phonetically irregular words (e.g. the, a, said) may appear frequently in the text. Through explicit instruction and practice, these high frequency words will become sight words for the children. Read, read, read. Review, review, review. Don't be afraid to practice. This practice builds fluency and confidence for the readers.

SUGGESTED PHONICS ACTIVITIES

Audience: Kindergarten–First Grade
Time Commitment: 25 percent of the reading/language arts block of time

1. Cup Sounds: Place several models of the sounds on a table. Quickly cover one of them with a cup. The child must identify the sound that you covered.
2. Hop Over: Using a small frog, bunny, etc., have the child hop over the letter after the teacher says its sound.
3. Circle-a-Sound: Form a circle with a piece of yarn. Have the child place a letter into the circle when the teacher says the sound.
4. Hide-the-Sound: The teacher hides a letter in each hand. The child tries to guess the letter by stating its sound. The teacher reveals the letter and checks for accuracy.
5. Paper Bag Sounds: Place several letters or pictures into a bag. The child selects one and states its beginning sound, medial or ending sound.
6. Pocket Chart Sounds: Sort pictures in the pocket chart by beginning, medial or ending sounds.
7. Buddy Phonics: Have students work in pairs and ask each other to show the letters for certain sounds and later to show words as they are asked.
8. Hear-a-Sound: As the teacher reads a book, children raise their hands each time they hear a word that begins with a certain sound. These words may then be recorded on a chart or chalkboard.
9. Dry-Erase Sounds: Children write dictated words and sentences on dry-erase boards. The teacher holds them accountable for accuracy.
10. Word Study Journals: Children cut and paste pictures according to their beginning, medial, ending sound or spelling pattern. Computer lists of words, generated according to spelling pattern may be included in this journal for reading, reference and review.
11. Magnetic Sounds: Place magnetic letters along the bottom of a magnetized board. Have several examples of each sound. Direct the children to move certain sounds to the top of the board. Later, they will be able to spell words by manipulating the letters on these boards.
12. Magazine Clips: Cut pictures from magazines according to the sounds being studied and glue them onto paper or into a book.

13. Puppet Stretch: The teacher uses a puppet to stretch sounds that the child then will write on a board or paper. This could be completed with isolated sounds or words.

Audience: Second Grade–Third Grade
Time Commitment: 25 percent of the reading/language arts block of time

1. Use any of the above-mentioned activities if there are nonreaders in the class.
2. Newspaper Mix: Cut letters from the newspaper to spell words of a particular pattern. Mixing a variety of fonts has an interesting visual appeal. Children should be able to read these words to the teacher.
3. Word Hunts: This activity could be completed as a whole class activity or a reading group activity. The teacher writes the spelling patterns on the board. Children hunt through books, magazines, and newspapers for words that fit the patterns they are studying. The teacher writes the words on the board as the children call them out. At the end of the activity, the pattern with the most words is the winner.
4. Word Study Bingo: Each child would be given a bingo grid. The spelling patterns would be written on the grid. Cover a space as the teacher calls a word with that pattern. A completed line is a winner. Extend this game by allowing the children to fill the grid with the spelling patterns or have spelling words written on the grid.
5. Tic-Tac-Toe: Provide pairs of children a grid on which they record the spelling words. As the teacher calls a word, the children take turns covering spaces. A completed line is a winner. Extend with blank grids. If child can orally spell the word the teacher calls, that child may cover a space.
6. Roll the Dice: Have one die with beginning sounds (onset) on it. Have another die with the vowel and ending of the spelling pattern (rime). Children take turns rolling the dice to see if they can make a word. When time is called, the child with the most words wins.
7. Word Races: Divide the class or reading group into two teams. As the teacher calls words to the teams, a player from each team must race to write the word on the board. Points go to the team that completes this task first. When time is called, the team with the most points wins.
8. Word Origins: Children of higher ability are learning about root words, prefixes and suffixes. Have the students search dictionaries for the ori-

gins of words and related words. The students are often surprised by what they find.

9. Speed Sorts: Using a stopwatch, time a child as a word sort is completed. Record the time and have the child try to beat that time on a repeated sort. Extend this activity by having children time each other.

10. Journal Search: Have the children reread their journal writings. Allow them to use a highlighter to mark any words that have the spelling pattern being studied.

Chapter Four

The Contextual Reading Component

The *Reading Their Way* approach promotes the application of skills. While phonological awareness and phonics are very important, skills practice alone will not create successful readers. Children must have many opportunities to apply the skills they are learning. They must have many opportunities to read. They must be immersed in good literature. Immediate and frequent application is crucial. This is true of beginning readers and fluent readers in all of the elementary grades.

In *Reading Their Way,* children are immediately immersed in books that have the spelling patterns being studied. Initially, these may be books that concentrate on the letters and sounds themselves, for example ABC books or pictures books for beginning sounds. As soon as they learn to blend the /at/ word family, they are presented with books that utilize this pattern. Some favorites for this are *The Cat on the Mat* (D.C. Heath Publishers); *Mat*, Set I, Bob Books (Scholastic); and *I Spy*, Dr. Maggie series (Creative Teaching Press). When reading these books the children have many opportunities to decode the /at/ pattern as well as build a few sight words. As children grow in their abilities, teachers should select books that allow the children to practice those spelling patterns and skills that are being studied. This policy applies to kindergarten through third-grade levels.

Early readers also are immersed in books that are predictable and repetitive. While these books may not be decodable, they offer opportunities to practice other skills. Comprehension, sight words and fluency can be enhanced by reading a variety of texts.

As students progress in reading they are involved in more and more content area reading. This is particularly true in grade three. These students are expected to be able to read the material by themselves and gather meaning from it. They are expected to navigate their way through headings and subheadings while gleaning the important information. The emphasis changes from learning to read to reading to learn.

Immersion in such reading is mandatory if success is to be attained. Practice really does make perfect—well, nearly perfect, anyway. Children in kindergarten through second grade need to be exposed to this type of text. Content area material may be read aloud by an adult. In some cases, the children in these grade levels will be able to read the nonfiction, expository texts themselves. Publishers are greeting us with more and more nonfiction books on early reading levels. This is great news for teachers. The earlier we can get children involved with expository text the better. Teachers in grade three can expand upon the knowledge gained in the earlier grades.

When children are asked to apply what they are learning, they realize why instructional time was spent on those skills. Words make a lot more sense to them than just sounds in isolation. However, they will see that they needed those isolated sounds to make the word. Likewise, sentences and stories make much more sense to them than words in isolation. Application gives children the chance to pull everything together.

BASALS VERSUS TRADE BOOKS

Much like the phonics versus whole language controversy, the basal versus trade book battle still rages. In this area, too, we need to reach a balance. Both types of books offer a great deal to our young readers.

Generally, basal readers contain themes that are familiar to the children. The children's prior knowledge can be utilized to build comprehension. The stories do lend themselves to prediction of outcomes and follow-up discussion.

To expose children to broader themes, teachers will need to secure trade books. These books are available in a variety of genres. Like basal readers, they may lend themselves to activities that access the students' prior knowledge. They certainly can present great opportunities for prediction of outcomes and follow-up discussion. Trade books offer a wonderful building ground for comprehension skills.

Basal readers usually offer controlled vocabulary. As children see the words again and again, these words become sight words. At times this controlled vocabulary seems stifling, but it does support our beginning readers.

Trade books can offer the rich language that is so supported by the whole language movement. This exposure to extended vocabulary is very stimulating for our students. It creates gains in reading as well as writing. The texts of some trade books are decodable, others rely more heavily on repetition and predictability of text. Teachers need to build a supply of both types of trade books to allow for practice of a broader range of skills.

Another positive aspect of basal readers is that school divisions usually purchase a copy for every child. Children love to hold the book as they read. They love to get a good, close-up look at the pictures. They love to take the books home to read to others. Purchasing books is a big investment and often school divisions are unable to supply as many trade books as basal readers. Building a supply of books is an ongoing endeavor. Once again, the children gain the most if we invest in both trade books and basal readers.

BOOK SELECTION

Selection of books is very important. How do teachers know which books are best for each child? Think of the purpose for the reading.

If the teacher hopes to increase the reading proficiency of a child, a book on that child's instructional level would be most appropriate. If the teacher wants to increase the child's reading speed or fluency, a book on that child's independent level would be most appropriate. If the reading will be handled as a group project, for example content area reading, where better readers may assist weaker readers, a book on the child's frustrational level may be appropriate. The understanding here is that someone will read to the child. Never ask a child to read a book that is on their frustrational level. Have someone read it to them instead and everyone can participate in discussions. If the teacher strives to build a child's listening comprehension, a book on any level would be appropriate since someone is reading to the child.

Administering an informal reading inventory (IRI) is an excellent way to determine a child's reading level. Generally, these inventories will recommend a 90 to 97 percent accuracy rate for the instructional level on the Word Recognition in Context inventory. An independent level would be considered above 97 percent accuracy. Below 90 percent accuracy would indicate a frustrational reading level.

Readers will make the most progress if their time is spent reading at the instructional level. They will benefit the greatest if this instruction occurs at a higher instructional level such as 95 percent accuracy. This is a strong instructional level and has the child on the "cutting edge." Keeping children on this edge will challenge them yet keep them at a level where they can be successful.

Too often teachers keep children at their independent level. This is a great "comfort zone." Teachers feel good about the students' reading. Children are not struggling. Everything seems fine; however, what are the children learning? Gains are made when a few mistakes are made. If we always keep children in their comfort zone, progress will be slower.

Reading at the independent level is a great way to build fluency and a bank of sight words. Reading on the independent level also would be recommended if the child has difficulty comprehending the material. The actual decoding of words would be easy so that more attention could be devoted to ascertaining the meaning of the passage.

It is important that all books be a "good fit" for the child. While the reading level is important, so is the interest level. Interest and motivation have a major influence on determining a "good fit."

The Five-Finger Test can indicate if the book is a "good fit." Have the child read a one-hundred-word passage, raising a finger for each mistake; if more than five mistakes are made, the book is too difficult. This is just a quick way of assessing a 95 percent instructional level and thus a "good, cutting-edge fit."

Basal readers and trade books often are leveled according to readability. Spelling patterns generally follow the readability levels. Many teachers create their reading groups according to results of spelling inventories. Usually, the basal text begins with short vowel spellings, then progresses to long vowels, blends, digraphs, and so on to higher level spellings. Thus, many of the words in the basal readers are decodable at the child's instructional level of reading or can be taught as sight words. Because the language of trade books is broader, teachers will not always find the predictability and control of the spelling patterns. Teachers need to become book spies and search for those titles that best suit the needs of the readers.

The reading level of a basal text is often indicated by the company. This is helpful to teachers who may not feel comfortable with leveling books on their own. However, all teachers should be cautioned about those reading levels. Sometimes they do not "fit" the child. Hence, the teacher's observation and judgment are always crucial. The child's prior knowledge, interest and skill level have a huge impact on successful reading, no matter the level of the books.

More and more companies are leveling their trade books. While this is very helpful, again teachers need to be careful when selecting books. Teachers know their children, whereas book companies do not.

For years, the Reading Recovery program has advocated the use of leveled books. Also, Gay Su Pinnell and Irene Fountas have published several excellent books on this topic (see appendix B). Their leveling guides are very accurate and contain the titles of many, many trade books. *Matching Books to Readers* by Fountas and Pinnell is an excellent resource. Many publishing companies now are issuing lists of the books they carry, by levels. These companies often correlate their titles to the basal Reading Recovery as well as the Fountas and Pinnell leveling guidelines.

READING TO CHILDREN

Children need to be exposed to quality literature. This may involve books that the teacher reads to the children or the students may read to themselves. Either way, the rich language and story fabric is shared with the children.

Big books are wonderful for whole group (K–3) read-alouds and discussion. Chapter books can be wonderful read-alouds for grades 1 through 3. Chapter books, with fewer pictures, provide great opportunities to build listening comprehension. Picture books are a splendid resource of read-alouds for all grade levels. A class library of picture books should be required in every classroom.

Teachers need to read their favorite books to their students every day. Enthusiasm is contagious. A love of reading will be conveyed. The children will hear fluency and a variety of genres can be shared in this manner. The time devoted to this type of instruction is just as important as the time spent on skills.

SUGGESTED READING ACTIVITIES

Audience: Kindergarten–First Grade
Time Commitment: 25 percent of reading/language arts block of time
(progress to 50 percent of time as children learn to read and need less
phonological awareness instruction)

1. Nursery Rhymes: Songs, chants and nursery rhymes are prime starting
   places for reading material. First, the teacher would model the reading
   and then ask the child to read. This can occur before the child is actually able to read, while memorizing is still the main strategy in use.
   Rhymes are also great for those who know how to read because they
   lend themselves well to skill and comprehension discussions.
2. Read-Alouds: Using a big book or picture book, the teacher reads to
   the class. Comprehension and skills are enhanced by discussion prior,
   during and following reading.
3. Shared Reading: Using a big book, the teacher reads to the class and
   the children chime in on choruses or other repetitive portions.
4. Choral Reading: The entire class or group reads the story together. This
   may be accomplished with a big book format or multiple copies of
   books.
5. Echo Reading: The teacher reads a page to the children and then the
   children read that same page. This may be accomplished with a big
   book format or multiple-copy books.
6. Buddy Reading: The teacher will assign the children in groups of two
   and the children take turns reading to each other. This may occur with
   the children alternating pages as they read. This may also occur with
   one child reading an entire book and then the other child reading that
   same book.
7. Guided Reading: This would occur within the reading group. The
   teacher assigns a text on the appropriate level for instruction. Preread-
   ing activities such as predicting and vocabulary discussion take place.
   Then the children actually read the book on their own, with the teacher
   there for support and assistance as difficulties are indicated. After reading, discussions to enhance comprehension and skills would be held.
8. D.E.A.R. Time: This is a time to Drop Everything And Read. Usually
   the reading materials are freely selected by the children. It is more of

a time to enjoy books than actually practice skills or build proficiency. Fifteen to twenty minutes is the recommended time frame. The whole class reads, even the teacher!

9. Reading Buddies: One class would be paired with another and they gather together perhaps once a week for buddy reading. Pairing classes from differing grade levels works well. The older children love to read to the younger ones and vice versa. It gives everyone a chance to practice reading and show off a little. Teachers can be reading buddies too.

10. Silent Sustained Reading: This type of reading should be scheduled every day. The material would be on the child's instructional level. It is best if this reading occurs as a follow-up to a child's reading group. It could be continued reading, such as in a chapter book, or it could be in the form of a rereading. Silent sustained reading is a great way to practice reading.

Audience: Second Grade–Third Grade
Time Commitment: 50 percent of the reading/language arts block of time

1. All of the above activities are appropriate, just with the higher instructional level material.

2. Reader's Theater: Children perform their reading before an audience. They do not have to memorize the words, rather they read from the text. Small motions and expressions are encouraged but the main emphasis is on the reading.

3. Sticky Note Reading: When reading in the content areas, the children use sticky notes to mark important parts or parts they question. These sticky notes direct the after-reading discussions between the child and teacher. This is recommended for building comprehension.

4. Research Readings: Children may be grouped according to ability or interests. Sometimes teachers group by mixed ability. In this case, materials on varying reading levels are provided. Each child is assigned certain material to read and information to gather. All of the information is compiled by the group and presented to the class.

5. Mixed Materials: Children benefit greatly from being required to work with many different types of reading material. Magazines, newspapers, and computers should be available as well as the customary basal readers and trade books.

Chapter Five

The Writing Component

Writing is the final component that completes the balance of instruction in *Reading Their Way*. As with reading, children are immediately immersed into writing. The connection between our spoken and written language is realized. The children are given opportunities to apply their knowledge and skills through writing. These opportunities enhance spelling, grammar, punctuation, handwriting, reading and comprehension. Multiple writing activities should be incorporated into every day's schedule. Just as more reading creates better readers, more writing creates better writers.

Through involvement in written language, children are able to practice and utilize their skills for encoding words. They must call upon their phonological awareness skills and phonics skills to spell the needed words. With daily practice and immersion beginning in kindergarten, the writing will progress from single words to complete stories, poems, plays, etc. This extended writing allows more practice and greater learning. Adams (1990) recommends that children be taught how to write individual letters from the start. This will enhance letter recognition and allow the children to write words as soon as the letters are introduced.

Data collected from kindergarten students who participated in *Reading Their Way* indicate that spelling achievement has been accelerated for those students. When these children leave kindergarten, the majority of them are spelling three-letter words correctly. In past years, our experience had been that these children would have control of beginning sounds only.

The *Reading Their Way* approach not only increases reading achievement but also spelling and writing achievement.

In kindergarten to second grade, children should be allowed and encouraged to utilize inventive spellings. This means asking the child to spell the words like they sound to them. The child is encouraged to take a risk and make a guess. A wise teacher then will take note of spelling errors as well as correct spellings. The errors show the teacher exactly what the child understands. The child's attempts at conventional spelling will indicate whether there is knowledge of letters, sounds and spelling patterns, etc. Spelling instruction should be driven by evidence gathered from writing samples as well as spelling tests. Instruction should be based on skill strengths. Focus lessons on what the child is using but confusing.

Figures 5.1, 5.2, and 5.3 are writing samples of a kindergarten child progressing through *Reading Their Way* instruction:

DAKoTA

[Dakota]
Figure 5.1.   Kindergarten Spelling Sample for Sept. 9, 1999.
Source: Kindergarten Writing Sample, Augusta County Public Schools (Fall 1999)

Sata Clos is up iN the ar

[Santa Claus is up in the air.]
Figure 5.2.   Kindergarten Spelling Sample for Dec. 21, 1999.
Source: Kindergarten Writing Sample, Augusta County Public Schools (Winter 1999)

for EStr I got a Sofst, Wit aNd a PeNcke rabet aNd I got a Choclit raBet.

[For Easter I got a soft, white and a pink rabbit
and I got a chocolate rabbit.]
Figure 5.3.   Kindergarten Spelling Sample for April 2000.
Source: Kindergarten Writing Sample, Augusta County Public Schools (Spring 2000)

While the inventive spellings are allowed, the teacher should insist on accountability as well. Once a child has shown knowledge of spelling patterns, the teacher should expect the child to correctly and consistently use that knowledge. The child should be asked to correct any errors that the teacher feels should not have been made.

Once children enter third grade, inventive spelling becomes less appropriate. By this point, most children do have control of many spelling patterns and should be held accountable for them. They have more strategies at their disposal and should not be allowed to spell words randomly. Often if children are not held accountable, they will just take the quick, easy way out and jot words down without a bit of thought. As with the younger children, spelling instruction in third grade is based on evidence gained from writing samples and spelling tests. Progress will be slow if accountability is not in place. Having high expectations for our writers will lead to the greatest gains.

Writing promotes the practice of syntactic (grammar) and semantic (meaning) skills. Children are learning to organize thoughts and convey meaning through writing. In kindergarten the writing may begin with dictations and single-word labels for pictures. As understandings develop, more complex sentences will be used. Children will become more aware of their choice of words and phrases. Conveying the message to their peers will become paramount.

More writing equates to better writing. Children deserve to be in classrooms that encourage lots of writing. This could happen in whole group settings, small group settings or with individuals. It might happen through shared writing, interactive writing or guided writing.

In shared writing, the teacher does the actual writing but discusses it with the class. By doing so, the children get to hear the teacher "think." The teacher demonstrates the use of our written language. Many opportunities arise to discuss letters and sounds. The entire writing process can be witnessed through the teacher's discussion with the class.

With interactive writing, the children participate with the teacher. There is joint thinking and problem solving. There is mutual participation in the actual writing of the text. The teacher and the children share control of the pen. Concepts of print are cultivated.

Writing also might be handled through a guided writing approach. This is often referred to as "writing workshop." Children are allowed free choice of topics or are given prompts. They take a piece of writing through the entire writing process, from prewriting to publishing. Conferences with the teacher and peers are important during this type of writing.

In these classrooms, the teacher has established an environment that promotes confidence and trust. By doing so, the teacher will notice the children are not as afraid of writing. They are not so worried about making a mistake. They feel freer to express themselves through writing.

As children are writing, they also are reading. They must read and reread their own pieces of writing to perfect them. The children listen as others read to them. Writing is a great way to achieve more reading practice. Clay (1985) has said that children practice many of the skills of reading in another form when they write. However, the writing must not just be copying letters or words from a chart or chalkboard. It must be going from thoughts to saying words to writing them. At least one study has shown that frequent opportunities to write using invented spellings enhance writing fluency. Over time daily writing experiences may be beneficial for children lacking phonemic awareness (Griffith and Klesius, 1990). When children write, they have to face head-on the problem of mapping spoken language onto written language. Serendipitous to this can be an understanding of the structure of spoken language, because the more children write, the better they become at segmenting sounds in words.

It is important that children see themselves as authors. They must have many opportunities to write but also many opportunities to share their completed works. Their stories, poems, plays, etc., need to be shared with an audience. The comments of their peers are very important to these budding authors. Successfully conveying their message is very important. Publish their pieces for all to enjoy.

To enhance successful writing, teach the children to follow the writing process. Model pre-writing strategies with them. Show them how to brainstorm topics, create story webs or use graphic organizers. Help them create a first draft and then confer with peers. Encourage editing and revising to improve writing. Finally, publish their works. Everyone likes to feel successful, and having a finished piece of work on display is a big pat on the back. Taking creative writing through the entire writing process does take time, but the outcome is well worth that time.

The writing component of *Reading Their Way* refers to creative writing. It does not refer to handwriting. Actually forming the letters is important, but it is viewed as a consequence and secondary to creative writing. Teachers in kindergarten through second grade usually teach manuscript handwriting. During the later portion of second grade, children often begin cursive handwriting and strive to improve that handwriting throughout the upper grades. Fifteen to twenty minutes a day should be spent on handwriting lessons when the children are in the introductory stages of learning manuscript and cursive. Once the skills have been taught, authentic application through creative writing is very beneficial.

Children enjoy using a variety of media for writing. Pencils, crayons, magic markers and chalk should be at their disposal. They love to write on paper, chalkboards and sidewalks. Computers are very powerful when writing. Overhead projectors are very stimulating as a writing surface. Be creative and vary your resources. The children will respond to your ingenuity.

Reading and writing should not be taught separately as there is such a relationship of mutual reciprocity. I once knew a lady whose daughter was moving to a foreign country. The mother told the daughter to call if she ever needed anything and that mother would be right there. "But, mom," said the daughter, "you don't know how to speak the language." "Then I'll write them a note," said the mom. While this story is humorous, it does show that the relationship between our spoken language and our written language is inseparable.

As this chapter concludes, it is important to remember that *Reading Their Way* is a balanced approach to literacy. It is vital to teach all components (phonemic awareness, phonics, contextual reading and writing). As stated in *Starting Out Right* by Burns, Griffin and Snow (1999), in the early grades the best reading programs offer a balance of elements, including reading for meaning and experiences with high-quality literature; intense, intentional and systematic instruction in phonics; and ample opportunities to read and write.

SUGGESTED WRITING ACTIVITIES

Audience: Kindergarten–First Grade
Time Commitment: 25 percent of the reading/language arts block of time

1. Picture Dictations: Teacher records the child's words below a picture.
2. Picture Labels: The child uses inventive spellings to label pictures. This may begin as one word and then progress to more words in the label.
3. Cards: The children illustrate cards for sick classmates, parents, etc., and add text to convey their message.
4. Journal Writing: Children are asked to write in their journal on a topic generated from a prompt or free choice writing. Each entry should be dated. Journals should be accompanied by a sharing time and response (oral and written) from the teacher. (Best if completed daily.)
5. Story Retellings: Children are asked to write a retelling of a story. This may be handled through shared writing, interactive writing or guided writing.
6. Story Innovations: Children are asked to create and write a new story based on the structure of a favorite story (e.g. Goldilocks and the Three Foxes).
7. New Ending: Children are asked to create and write a different ending for a favorite story.
8. Story Writing: Children are asked to use the writing process to create and write their own story.
9. Flap Art: Children fold a sheet of paper lengthwise and cut the top flap into four sections. Draw the character, setting, plot, solution. Add explanatory text under each flap.
10. Magic Words: Teachers dictate words and children write them on dry erase boards, erasing them like magic to make room for new words. In this case the children should be held accountable for the spellings. Extend by writing sentences.
11. Riddles: Children can be taught the steps in composing riddles and enjoy writing their own for classmates to solve.
12. Dignitary Writing: Individuals or the whole class can compose letters to famous persons, for example, the president of the United States. Often a response will be received.

Audience: Second Grade–Third Grade
Time Commitment: 25 percent of the reading/language arts block of time

1. Include all of the above activities, based on student needs.
2. Predictions: Children are asked to write predictions of what will happen in a story. Extend upon further reading by written responses to these predictions—confirm or change the prediction.
3. Reactions: Children write their reaction to a character, story plot, etc. Follow with group discussions of these reactionary writings.
4. Writing workshop: Give each child a folder to store his or her writings as they work through the entire writing process. This workshop should occur four to five days a week. Conferences and sharing are imperative in this workshop atmosphere.
5. Best Seller Check-Out: As children publish books, allow classmates to check them out for take-home reading.
6. Journal Search: Children review their journal writings from several weeks and determine if there are any consistent themes. If so, these may be topics for future writings.
7. Want Ads: Children write an ad for the hiring of a teacher or an item that they would like to purchase.
8. Pen Pals: Pair classes from the same school or other schools in your area. These children should write once a month and perhaps take a joint field trip to enable them to meet one another.
9. Character Pen Pals: Children can write to the character of a book. A teacher, serving the part of the character, would respond in writing. These writings could be sent via e-mail.
10. Author Letters: Individuals or the whole class could write to an author. Often a response is received.

Chapter Six

Comprehension

Yes, we have reached our ultimate goal, comprehension! *Webster's New Collegiate Dictionary* defines *comprehend* as "to grasp the nature, significance or meaning of." Reading comprehension is the ability to construct meaning from text. This is the purpose of reading. Why teach children to read, if they cannot understand what they read? Why teach children to read, if they cannot apply what they read to other situations? "We cannot discuss reading comprehension without acknowledging that a good reader is nothing less than a good thinker. In fact, decoding words, which for some children is a major accomplishment in itself, doesn't begin to describe the complete act of reading" (Wasserstein, 2000/2001, pgs. 74–77).

Some children can learn to decode text, but not comprehend. They are wonderful "word callers." This is not our goal in *Reading Their Way*. We are striving to develop fluent, strategic readers who can comprehend and use the knowledge gained from their reading.

A wonderful resource on reading comprehension is *Strategies That Work* by Stephanie Harvey and Anne Goudvis (2000). In this book they talk of strategies used by proficient readers. An interpretation of these strategies follows:

Connections with prior knowledge: Understanding is enhanced when children can connect the text to their own experiences and lives.
Asking questions: Understanding is enhanced when children are encouraged to ask questions about the text. If children are asking questions, they are actively engaged with the text. Teachers love to hear correct

answers, but they should also love to hear probing questions from students.

Visualizing: Understanding is enhanced when children create visual images in their minds as they read. Once again, they are making connections to their own experiences.

Drawing inferences: Understanding is enhanced when children can take clues from the text and predict what will happen. It is interesting to watch the advancement of their inferences from some that may be illogical to more sophisticated inferences that are completely logical.

Determining important ideas: Understanding is enhanced when children can filter important ideas from fluff. Ask beginning readers to highlight the important information in a selection of text; they will highlight everything. This is a skill that needs to be taught and developed through lots of practice.

Synthesizing information: Understanding is enhanced when a child can take new information gained from text and create something original from it.

Repairing understanding: Understanding is enhanced when children realize that comprehension has been interrupted and utilize some strategies to correct that situation. Re-reading is a strategy frequently used to solve this problem.

The ability to decode words is required for success in all content areas. Reading comprehension is obviously also a must for success. In kindergarten through second grade, most of the reading comprehension occurs with story. However, once children enter third grade, the emphasis changes to more reading in the content areas. Now reading comprehension deals with literature as well as content area, nonfiction material. In *Reading Their Way* we begin building comprehension skills in kindergarten, with a stronger emphasis on nonfiction material beginning in second grade.

The foundation of comprehension skills is built in kindergarten. These skills should be reinforced and expanded upon during each subsequent year in school. Like so many skills, proficiency will improve if we begin instruction early and require children to frequently apply the skills of comprehension.

Teacher modeling of strategies is very important. Begin with an explanation and demonstration of the strategy. It is advantageous for teachers to "talk through" their own thinking as they demonstrate the strategy to the class. For instance, a teacher may say, "Oh, I didn't understand what I just read. I better read that again."

Opportunities to apply the strategies must occur frequently. This could be through guided practice, where the teacher and the children share in the practice. In guided practice, the teacher would support the child as a new skill is attempted.

Application of skills could also occur during independent level work. After the guided practice, the children may be ready to try the strategies on their own. Still, feedback is needed from the teacher.

In earlier chapters, we talked of keeping children on the cutting edge. This is also true of developing comprehension skills. Support children as they are progressing, but not to the point that learning is no longer challenging for the child. Encourage them to demonstrate strategies in more difficult text, as appropriate. Independence is the goal.

Prediction is a great comprehension strategy to begin instructing in kindergarten. The teacher could display a big book version of *The Gingerbread Man*. Read the title to the children and ask them to look at the picture on the cover. Next ask them to predict what they think will happen in this story. Accept all responses because this will build the confidence of the children. Some rather shy students may be afraid to venture a prediction if they think it might be wrong. Thus, accepting all responses is important.

It is also important to ask why they made that particular prediction. Explanations add to understanding. If conflicting predictions occur, this is great. Often the discussion from such conflict is quite beneficial. Children should be encouraged to give their reasoning for their predictions.

Next, take a "picture walk" through the book. Ask the children to explain what is happening in the pictures. Talk about any unusual vocabulary in the book. Ask them if they want to keep their predictions or if they want to change something. Again, always ask why they think that prediction is accurate. It is preferable that they can substantiate their predictions with text. Did the character say something that led the student to that prediction? Perhaps a picture led the student to their prediction. Students should be held accountable to text.

Last, the story should be read by the children or to the children, checking on those predictions. The teacher should pre-read the book so that appropriate stopping points are marked and predictions can be reassessed at those points. Discussion should be held at the end of the book to check on comprehension of the story. The teacher could ask such questions as:

1. Did the story end the way you expected?
2. Have you ever done anything like the characters in this story?
3. Which character was your favorite and why?
4. How could this story have ended differently?
5. Have you read any books similar to this one? How were they similar?
6. Why do you think that character acted that way? Would you?

Predicting can begin on the first day of kindergarten. It could be implemented every day during guided reading or shared reading. This is a strategy that should be utilized at all grade levels, kindergarten through third grade. As children get older and more proficient in their reading and writing the format for predicting might change, but the strategy is highly recommended for all grade levels.

As children mature, they may be asked to put their predictions in writing. As they read longer books, they may be asked to predict what is going to happen in the next chapter, rather than on the next page. All children should be required to substantiate their predictions with text. This is a wonderful way to hold them accountable to text.

Good readers are strategic readers, meaning they have strategies to implement as they read. They utilize the comprehension strategies supported by Harvey and Goudvis. These readers do visualize when reading; they do ask questions; they do make inferences and synthesize information.

Strategic readers do understand the structure of the text. They know to look for organizational patterns. They have a plan that helps them navigate their way through the text. It is the teacher's responsibility to teach this plan to the students. Beginning in second grade, children should be interacting with the chapter title, subtitles, and subheadings. They should be aware that many informational materials include a summary section at the end of the chapter. As students learn to recognize these structural patterns, they can organize the information more efficiently and effectively.

Do you ask your students questions? Do you ask them the *right* questions? Oh, that's a good question. "The depth of student comprehension resides almost exclusively with the rigor of the questions that teachers ask. If students are asked to respond to literal questions of 'who' and 'what' rather than 'why' or 'what if,' their level of understanding will stagnate" (Wasserstein, pgs. 74–77).

Sticky notes can be a teacher's best friend. Teachers and students can use the sticky notes to indicate passages that they relate to from prior experiences, have questions about, answer questions, or include vocabulary that is determined to be important. Sticky notes could be used for short rewrites of passages. There are multiple uses for sticky notes when teaching comprehension. Schools should definitely invest in these for their teachers and students.

Following are various comprehension activities that have been proven effective in classrooms. The appropriate grade level is indicated. Each activity also includes an indication of the comprehension skills addressed by that activity. The code for the comprehension skills is: PK=Prior Knowledge; Q=Questioning; V=Visualizing; I=Inferences; II=Important Ideas; S=Synthesizing; R=Repair understanding.

SUGGESTED COMPREHENSION ACTIVITIES

Audience: Kindergarten–First Grade
Time: Throughout the entire reading/language arts block and all content area blocks of time as reading/language arts are integrated

1. Predictions: Ask the children to look at the pictures/title and predict what will happen in the story. As they read, they find evidence that validates or invalidates the prediction. PK, Q, I, II, S
2. Brainstorming: Children are asked to think of many different answers to a theme-related question posed by the teacher. These brainstorming ideas may be recorded on charts for future reference and discussion. This activity may occur with the whole group, small groups, or individuals. PK, V, II
3. Connection Discussions: Class discussions that tap into the children's prior knowledge are encouraged. The purpose is to help the children make connections between their lives and the story, etc. PK, Q, V, I, II, S
4. Graphic Organizers: This is a graphic, visual representation of information from the text. Many examples are available from a variety of sources. A graphic organizer may be completed as a whole group activity or small groups or individuals. PK, Q, V, I, II, S
5. Sketch the Meaning: Children are asked to draw a picture to represent what the story means to them. PK, V, S
6. Metacognition: Teachers should "think aloud" as they are reading and working with text. This allows the children to hear the teacher's thinking processes. The children can see what the teacher does when an unknown word or concept is encountered. PK, Q, V, I, II, S, R
7. Retelling: Children orally retell the story; the teacher is observing accuracy of information, sequence and use of important terminology. S
8. Rereading: A strategy used by fluent readers when comprehension is interrupted. This is a great way to repair understanding. R
9. Riddles: Children compose riddles, with three clues. They read their riddles to the class. This is a wonderful comprehension builder for the child composing the riddle as well as the listener who is trying to solve the riddle. V, I, II, S

Audience: Second Grade–Third Grade

Time: Throughout the reading/language arts block and all content area blocks of time as reading/language arts are integrated

1. All of the above—these are excellent strategies for all grade levels.
2. Opinion Questions: During the pre-reading time, have the children state or write their opinions on the subject matter included in the passage. During reading, they read to see if their opinion agrees with that of the author. PK, I, S
3. Easing the Challenge: Begin instruction of a theme or content area with books at an easy reading level and progress to books that are more challenging. PK, R
4. Textbook Overview: Preview the text structure with a "walk through" discussion. Point out such features as table of contents, glossary, chapter titles, subtitles, index, etc. This helps children to see how the information is organized. V, II, R
5. Textbook Scavenger Hunt: A game where children are asked to look for certain information in the table of contents, index, glossary, etc. This enhances their understanding of the organization of the book and its information. V, II, R
6. Expectation Outlines: Children preview the text and then formulate three questions that they predict will be answered by the text. These questions can then be organized by similarities and put into an outline form. This is an activity for the whole class, small groups, or individuals. Q, I, II, S
7. K-W-L: Children record the "K—what they know about the topic; W—what they want to know about the topic; L—what they learned about the topic." This activity is strong because it involves thinking during the pre-reading stage, during the reading stage, and the post-reading stage. PK, Q, I, II, S
8. Categorize Vocabulary: This is an activity where children list words that pertain to a topic (self-generated or from the text). Next they categorize the words by similarities. I, II, S
9. W-W-W: Write, Write, Write—children are given two to three minutes to freely write about a topic. They write constantly during this time, including anything they know about the topic. Discussion is held at the end of this free writing time. This is usually considered a pre-reading

activity, although it could occur during or post-reading as well. Q, V, I, II, S

10. Header Questions: Children rewrite section headings into a question format and then read for answers to those questions. Q, I, S

11. Think-Pair-Share: Children think about the text, next they are paired with a classmate, and finally they share their thoughts with each other. This is a wonderful cooperative learning activity. The Think-Pair-Share can conclude as a group sharing time. PK, Q, V, I, II, S, R

12. Do You Agree?: Ask the class to vote on whether they agree with the author. The children should be able to substantiate their reasoning. PK, I, S

13. Mark It: When children encounter important information, they highlight, underline, or make notes in the margin. PK, Q, V, I, II, S, R

14. Tic-Tac-Toe: An activity to review vocabulary; children record vocabulary words onto a tic-tac-toe grid and then cover their words as the teacher calls out the definition, or the teacher may call on a child to give the definition; this may be played as teacher against the class or by pairs of students. PK, V, R

15. Two-Column Notes: Children divide their paper into two columns; they record their questions in one column; they record the answers to those questions in the other column. Q

16. Five Senses: Children describe the text, using the five senses (i.e. what they see, hear, feel, smell and taste). V

17. Mystery Word: Child holds a word card that only the classmates can see; the classmates must give clues to the meaning of the word and see if the card holder can determine the word. I

18. Concluding Questions: Children read the summary questions first and then read the text for the purpose of answering those questions. II

19. Rewrite: Children rewrite the story in their own words; teacher observes accuracy, sequence and use of important terms. S

20. Innovate on Text: Children rewrite the story by keeping the same story structure but using different characters, setting, etc. S

Chapter Seven

Time Schedules
and Lesson Designs

"How can I get everything done in a day?"

"I could teach these children if I had more time."

"I could really accelerate progress if I didn't have so many students."

These are statements often uttered by teachers faced with the demands of everyday teaching. In today's world, with division curriculum requirements, state testing mandates, larger schools, and societal pressures, teachers are often frustrated. Teaching is a demanding career and "getting everything done" is a challenge, even for the most experienced, dedicated teacher.

"One of the major revelations of the 1990s has been that when 'boiled down,' the actual amount of instructional time available in a traditionally scheduled school day is alarmingly brief (National Education Commission on Time and Learning, 1994). Because of the time lost to class opening, closings, interruptions, and various noninstructional activities, the actual class time available for instruction is far less than the allotted period. Consequently, teachers faced with limited time often feel pressed, at the very least, to *expose* children to curriculum. . . . Perhaps one of the most critical issues facing schools regarding the allocation of time is the indisputable fact that some students need more time to learn than others" (Canady and Rettig, 1996, pg. 4).

The range of student achievement found in classrooms, with the inclusion of children who have various physical, emotional and educational needs, requires that we move to different education models from those of the past (International Reading Association, 2000). In Augusta County, Virginia, we have found a way to create more time for instruction, without lengthening the school day. We have implemented parallel block scheduling as developed by Robert Lynn Canady, Professor Emeritus, University of Virginia, Charlottesville, Virginia. We were fortunate to have Dr. Canady serve as a consultant to the Augusta County School division as we implemented this scheduling.

Parallel block scheduling allows teachers to instruct small reading/language arts groups of homogeneous ability. It promotes the use of extension centers where the students engage in remedial or enrichment activities that supplement the classroom instruction. It creates an environment where the children are always able to interact with an adult. There is always someone working directly with the children during this reading/language arts block.

"Because instruction occurs continually for all students throughout the entire time block, the total amount of teacher-directed instruction is significantly increased. Additionally, classroom teachers can teach without the disruption and fragmentation caused by students being pulled out during direct instruction periods" (Canady, 1990).

Parallel block scheduling has been implemented in nine of the twelve schools in Augusta County, with plans to implement in all of the schools over the next year. The schedule varies from school to school, based on the unique needs of that building. Each was developed around the Master Block Specials Cycle and Planning Schedule, as developed by Robert Lynn Canady. Figure 7.1 illustrates this scheduling grid. Figures 7.2 and 7.3 depict completed examples from two sites.

We began in two schools, utilizing parallel block in kindergarten and first grades. Class rolls were set to create two ability groups in each homeroom, one a higher ability group and one a lower ability group. For instance, if there were three sections of a grade level, six groupings were needed. Group #1 was the highest ability group and Group #6 was the lowest ability group. We arranged the following pairings for the homerooms: Group #1 with Group #4; Group #2 with Group #5; Group #3 with Group #6. This pairing would allow portions of the day with a heterogeneous grouping and portions of the day with homogeneous grouping for instruction. This pairing also avoided the combining of the highest group with the lowest group, where their diverse needs would have been difficult to manage. Figures 7.4 and 7.5 illustrate two rubrics that were developed to assist teachers and principals in establishing the groups.

	I	II	III	IV	V	VI	VII	VIII
Kindergarten								Plan Cycle
Grade 1							Plan Cycle	
Grade 2					Plan Cycle			
Grade 3				Plan Cycle				
Grade 4			Plan Cycle					
Grade 5		Plan Cycle						
Specials	Plan	Grade 5	Grade 4	Grade 3	Grade 2	Lunch	Grade 1	Kindergarten

Figure 7.1. Master Block Specials Cycle and Planning Schedule
Source: Canady, Robert Lynn, "Using Parallel Block Scheduling Strategies in Elementary Schools" (2000)

	8:40–9:25	9:25–10:10	10:15–11:00	11:05–11:50	11:50–12:35	12:35–1:20	1:25–2:10	2:15–3:00
Kindergarten	Whole Class LA & Integrated Curr.		Reading Their Way Groups/ Extension Centers		Lunch 12:21–12:51 Lunch 12:24–12:54 Lunch 12:27–12:57			Planning
First Grade	Reading Their Way Groups/ Extension Centers		Whole Class LA & Integrated Curr.		Lunch 12:12–12:42 Lunch 12:15–12:45 Lunch 12:15–12:48		Planning	Enrichment/ Remediation
Second Grade					Lunch 11:51–12:21 Lunch 11:54–12:24 Lunch 12:00–12:30	Planning		Enrichment/ Remediation
Third Grade			Planning		Lunch 12:03–12:33 Lunch 12:06–12:36 Lunch 12:09–12:39			Enrichment/ Remediation
Fourth Grade			Planning	Lunch 11:42–12:12 Lunch 11:45–12:15 Lunch 11:48–12:18				Enrichment/ Remediation
Fifth Grade		Planning		Lunch 11:30–12:00 Lunch 11:33–12:03 Lunch 11:36–12:06				Enrichment/ Remediation
Specialists	Planning				Lunch			

Figure 7.2.   Parallel Block in Kindergarten and First Grade

Source: Augusta County Public Schools (2000)

| | 8:15-8:30 | 8:30-9:15 | 9:15-10:00 | 10:00-10:45 | 10:45-11:30 | 11:30-12:15 | 12:15-1:00 | 1:00-1:45 | 1:45-2:30 | 2:30-2:52 |
		I	II	III	IV	V	VI	VII	VIII	
Kind.	Opening Activities	Whole Class Inst. L/A	Whole Class Inst. L/A	Small Group Reading	Small Group Reading	Lunch	Math	Science, Social Studies	Planning	Ending Activities & SOL Remed. or Enrichment
Grade 1	Opening Activities	Small Group Reading	Small Group Reading	Whole Class Inst. L/A	Whole Class Inst. L/A	Math	Lunch	Planning	Science, Social Studies	Ending Activities & SOL Remed. or Enrichment
Grade 2	Opening Activities	Math, SC, SS, & Extension	Math, SC, SS, & Extension	Math, SC, SS, & Extension	Planning	Lunch	L/A, W/S, R/W, & Extension	L/A, W/S, R/W, & Extension	L/A, W/S, R/W, & Extension	Ending Activities & SOL Remed. or Enrichment
Grade 3	Opening Activities	L/A, W/S, R/W, & Extension	L/A, W/S, R/W, & Extension	L/A, W/S, R/W, & Extension	Math, SC, SS, & Extension	Planning	Lunch	Math, SC, SS, & Extension	Math, SC, SS, & Extension	Ending Activities & SOL Remed. or Enrichment
Grade 4	Opening Activities	Math, SC, SS, & Rotation	Math, SC, SS, & Rotation	Planning	Lunch	Math, SC, SS, & Rotation	Language Arts	Language Arts	Language Arts	Ending Activities & SOL Remed. or Enrichment

Figure 7.3. Parallel Block in Kindergarten–Third Grade

(continued)

	8:15-8:30	8:30-9:15	9:15-10:00	10:00-10:45	10:45-11:30	11:30-12:15	12:15-1:00	1:00-1:45	1:45-2:30	2:30-2:52
		I	II	III	IV	V	VI	VII	VIII	
Grade 5	Opening Activities	Math, SC, SS, & Rotation	Planning	Math, SC, SS, & Rotation	Lunch	Math, SC, SS, & Rotation	Language Arts	Language Arts	Language Arts	Ending Activities & SOL Remed. or Enrichment
Resource Classes (P.E., Music, Guidance, Library)	Opening Activities	Planning	Grade 5	Grade 4	Grade 2	Grade 3	Lunch	Grade 1	Kind.	Ending Activities & SOL Remed. or Enrichment

Legend
L/A = Language Arts
SC = Science
SS = Social Studies
W/S = Word Study
R/W = Reading/Writing
Extension = ½ Class size initial instruction

Head Start
Tues. = Music
W = Guidance (every other week)
Thurs. = P.E.

Early Childhood Special Education
M = Library
W = Guidance (every other week)
Thurs. = P.E.

Figure 7.3. Parallel Block in Kindergarten–Third Grade *(continued)*

Source: Augusta County Public Schools (2000)

READING THEIR WAY
RUBRIC FOR ORGANIZING CLASSROLLS
OF UPCOMING FIRST GRADE CHILDREN

Child's Name: _____

Teacher's Name: _____

Reading Proficiency:	Points (Check One)
*1.1 level reader or higher (indicate level _____)	4 _____
*PP3 level reader	3 _____
*PP2 level reader	2 _____
*PP1 or below (Bob Books, Sunshine, etc.)	1 _____
Word Study (Phonics) Proficiency:	
*WW or higher and spells quickly and correctly on their own	4 _____
*Knows *at least* 23 sounds; LN speller with short vowels	3 _____
*Knows *at least* 15 sounds; ELN speller w/beginning & ending sounds	2 _____
*Knows fewer than 15 sounds and weak speller	1 _____
Writing Proficiency:	
*More than 3 sentences written easily and independently	4 _____
*Three sentences but slower process	3 _____
*Fewer than 3 sentences; requires lots of teacher support	2 _____
*Labors over creative writing	1 _____
Work Habits:	
*Highly motivated; chooses reading as an independent activity	4 _____
*Enjoys reading but would not choose as independent activity	3 _____
*Tolerates reading group	2 _____
*Unmotivated/Uninterested in language arts activities	1 _____
TOTAL POINTS:	

Figure 7.4.

Source: Augusta County Public Schools (2000)

READING THEIR WAY
RUBRIC FOR ORGANIZING CLASSROLLS
OF UPCOMING SECOND GRADE CHILDREN

Child's Name: _____

Teacher's Name: _____

Reading Proficiency:	Points (Check One)
*2.2 level reader or higher (indicate level _____)	4 _____
*2.1 level reader	3 _____
*1.2 level reader	2 _____
*Lower than 1.2 level reader (indicate level _____)	1 _____
Word Study (Phonics) Proficiency:	
*WW/SJ; r-controlled vowels, homophones, doubling	4 _____
*WW: typical long vowel patterns correct	3 _____
*Proficient with sounds; LN; short vowels correct, blends, diagraphs	2 _____
*Knows *at least* 23 sounds; LN; short vowel substitutions	1 _____
Writing Proficiency:	
*More than 5 sentences written easily and independently	4 _____
*Five sentences but slower process	3 _____
*Fewer than 5 sentences; requires lots of teacher support	2 _____
*Labors over creative writing	1 _____
Work Habits:	
*Highly motivated; chooses reading as an independent activity	4 _____
*Enjoys reading but would not choose as independent activity	3 _____
*Tolerates reading group	2 _____
*Unmotivated/Uninterested in language arts activities	1 _____
TOTAL POINTS:	

Figure 7.5.

Source: Augusta County Public Schools (2000)

The schedule was constructed with a 90-minute block of time designated for whole class instruction in reading/language arts. Two 45-minute blocks were also created. One 45-minute block of time was for the homogeneous, small group reading/language arts instruction with the classroom teacher. The other 45-minute block of time was designated for instruction in an extension center.

Every school makes use of their reading specialist as the leader of one extension center. This specialist is paired with a para-educator to create an appropriate pupil-teacher ratio. The activities conducted in this extension center reinforce or enrich the classroom instruction. Schools without reading specialists should reexamine their needs because reading specialists provide leadership and instructional expertise for the prevention and remediation of reading difficulties (Snow, Burns and Griffin, 1998).

Another extension center may be a computer lab. This is manned by one or two para-educators. These para-educators have been trained in working with groups of children in a computer lab situation. Just as with the reading specialist extension center, the activities in the computer lab reinforce or enrich the classroom instruction.

Some schools do not have a computer lab available for use as an extension center. At these sites we assigned two para-educators to work with the children in another available classroom, thus creating an extension center. As stated before, the activities in this extension center reinforced or enriched the classroom instruction.

In designing the schedule, we set the first 90 minutes of the day as kindergarten's whole group reading/language arts instructional time. At the end of the 90 minutes, they would begin small group instruction and extension centers. To create the small groups, the teacher divides the class (remember the rolls were planned for a high group and a low group) and one group (or approximately one-half of the class) stays with the classroom teacher while the other half goes to extension. After a 45-minute block of instruction, these groups switch and the extension group receives small group instruction from the classroom teacher. The group that had been with the classroom teacher would enter extension. This same time scheduling model was utilized with first grade, except they entered extension centers while kindergarten children were in their 90-minute block of whole class instruction (see figure 7.6).

90-MINUTE BLOCK SCHEDULE
FOR KINDERGARTEN AND FIRST GRADE

(A Sample upon Which to Build in Other Grade Levels)

Kindergarten

8:30–10:00	10:00–10:45	10:45–11:30
Whole Group Reading/LA	Small Group & Extension	Small Group & Extension

First Grade

8:30–9:15	9:15–10:00	10:00–11:30
Small Group & Extension	Small Group & Extension	Small Group & Extension

Figure 7.6.
Source: Augusta County Public Schools (2000)

By arranging the schedule in this manner we were able to utilize the same personnel in extension centers for both grade levels. Extension centers are very important and should not be considered a "down time" or "play time." This is a structured environment that contributes greatly to the accelerated progress of the students. As Cunningham et al.'s research (1999) supports, schools need to provide additional support for children who struggle and additional challenges for children who comprehend skills and material quickly.

Most schools have enjoyed alternating which extension center the child enters. For example, one day the group will attend the computer lab and the next day that group will be with the reading specialist. The following day they return to the computer lab and so on. This ensures that the child is receiving instruction from the classroom teacher and the reading specialist as well as the para-educators. The children benefit greatly from the multiple opportunities to practice their skills in a variety of ways. This schedule allows for lots of review and support. It also provides opportunities for lots of enrichment. Individual needs of children can be addressed using this model. Figure 7.7 illustrates a schedule where extension centers are alternated between days.

Day 4

	Groups	8:30-10:00	10:00-10:45	10:45-11:30
K	A,B	A,B	A	B
K	C,D	C,D	C	D
K	E,F	E,F	E	F
Reading Resource		First Grade	B	A
Extension Center		First Grade	D,F	C,E

Day 5

	Groups	8:30-10:00	10:00-10:45	10:45-11:30
K	A,B	A,B	A	B
K	C,D	C,D	C	D
K	E,F	E,F	E	F
Reading Resource		First Grade	D	C
Extension Center		First Grade	F,B	E,A

Day 6

	Groups	8:30-10:00	10:00-10:45	10:45-11:30
K	A,B	A,B	A	B
K	C,D	C,D	C	D
K	E,F	E,F	E	F
Reading Resource		First Grade	F	E
Extension Center		First Grade	B,D	A,C

Figure 7.7. Kindergarten Extension Center Schedule
Source: Augusta County Public Schools (2000)

"Consider the benefits of this type of scheduling, particularly for at-risk or low-achieving students:

- All students receive equal instructional time in reading
- All students receive teacher-directed instruction unbroken by pullouts
- All students are taught in both homogeneous and heterogeneous groupings during the school day
- All students have less unsupervised seatwork activities
- All students receive increased small-group instructional time in reading."

Source: "Parallel Block Scheduling: A Better Way to Organize a School" by Robert Lynn Canady, *Principal,* pgs. 34–36, January 1990.

Communication between the classroom teacher and the extension teachers is critical. The extension teachers must know which skills the classroom teacher is focusing upon each week. All teachers and paraeducators must share insights into the progress of the children. Our teachers jointly plan with the extension teachers at least once a week. Often written communication is shared among the personnel. Ongoing communication also occurs before school, after school, and during lunch as needed.

Most of our schools have the reading/language arts block in the morning. For example, it is typical that extensions for first grade begin at 8:30 a.m. The class is divided by groups, with approximately one-half staying with the classroom teacher for 45 minutes and the other half going to extension for that 45 minutes. At 9:15 a.m. those groups trade places, ensuring that everyone is receiving instruction by the classroom teacher as well as extension center instruction. This rotation would conclude at 10:00 a.m. At that time, the first grade children would begin their 90-minute whole class instruction of reading/language arts.

Kindergarten children would have been involved with their 90-minute whole class instruction from 8:30 a.m. to 10:00 a.m. At this point they are ready for the small group/extension center rotation. This rotation would conclude at 11:30 a.m.

Science, Social Studies/Health, and language arts are integrated throughout the day. Generally there is a separate block of time for math instruction. Kindergarten teachers also feel strongly about the importance of including free-choice centers sometime during the day.

See figures 7.8, 7.9, and 7.10 for samples of kindergarten classroom schedules. Figures 7.11, 7.12, and 7.13 illustrate first grade scheduling options that have proven successful. Figure 7.14 details specific activities and time options during the language arts blocks for these grades. Figure 7.15 outlines suggested time allotments for each of the *Reading Their Way* component parts, kindergarten through third grade.

	Monday	Tuesday	Wednesday	Thursday	Friday
8:30 8:45	Unpack, Table Activities, Moment of Silence, Transition to Group Time				
8:45 9:15	Good Morning Songs, Pledge, Story Time, Big Book, Group Sharing Time				
9:15 10:15	Whole Group–Language Arts, Math Their Way, Calendar Activities, Alphabet, Language Experience Themes, Writing, Reading Their Way				
10:15 11:00	Reading Their Way & Extension Session 1				
11:00 11:45	Reading Their Way & Extension Session 2				
11:45 12:15	Physical Education or Unit Study				
12:15 12:25	Wash Hands & Bathroom Break				
12:25 12:55	Lunch				
12:55 1:20	Math				
1:20 2:05	Day 1–P.E. Day 6–P.E.	Day 2–Comp. Lab Day 7–Library	Day 3–Guidance Day 8–Math	Day 4–Music Day 9–Math	Day 5–Library Day 10–Music
2:05 2:45	Rest Time or Choice or Unit Study				
2:45 2:55	Pack-Up				
2:55 3:30	Dismissal				

Figure 7.8.   Kindergarten Schedule

Source: Augusta County Public Schools (2000)

	Monday	Tuesday	Wednesday	Thursday	Friday
8:30 8:40	Announcements, Pledge, School Pledge, Lunch Count				
8:40 9:15	Songs, Calendar, Number Line, Weather, Morning Message, Integrated Math, Language Arts, Science, Social Studies Unit Study				
9:15 9:40	Journal Writing	Integrated Science, Social Studies, Poem Books	Journal Writing	Integrated Science, Social Studies, Poems Books	Journal Writing
9:40 10:00	Phonemic Awareness				
10:00 10:10	Snack				
10:10 11:40	10:10-10:55 – Reading Group A (Reading Their Way) Reading Group B in Extension Lab 10:55-11:40 – Reading Group B (Reading Their Way) Reading Group A in Extension Lab				
11:40 12:00	Story, Bathroom Break, Transition				
12:00 12:30	Lunch				
12:30 1:00	Recess				
1:00 1:30	Rest Time (1st six weeks) Centers: Math, Science, Puzzles, Computer, Writing				
1:30 2:20	Specials				
2:20 3:00	Math	Math	Math	Math	Ice Cream Show & Tell
3:00 3:30	Dismissal				

Figure 7.9. Kindergarten Schedule

Source: Augusta County Public Schools (2000)

	Monday	Tuesday	Wednesday	Thursday	Friday
8:30 8:45	Attendance, Lunch Count, Pledge, Moment of Silence, Helpers, Group Time: Math Their Way, Calendar Activities, Weather Graph, Morning Message, ABC Song Activity				
8:45 9:20	Reading Their Way Instructional Group - Bluebirds				
9:20 10:00	Reading Their Way Instructional Group - Redbirds				
10:00 10:35	Math	Release Time/ Activity Time Games	Math	Math	Unit Study/ Show & Tell
10:35 10:45	Wash Hands/Bathroom Break				
10:45 11:00	Group Time, Unit Books, Songs, Discussions				
11:00 11:30	Lunch				
11:30 11:45	Activity Time Directions				
11:45 12:40	Activity Time: Students choose from various learning centers while teachers instruct students in small groups or individually on writing, reading skills, math skills, art, fine motor skills, phonemic awareness, word study & assessment				
12:40 12:50	Wash Hands/Bathroom Break				
12:50 1:00	Physical Education/Outside Playground				
1:00 1:45	Rest Time & Music Appreciation				
1:45 2:30	Specialist	Day 1–Gym Day 2–Music Day 3–Gym	Day 4–Computer Day 5–Guidance Day 6–Gym	Day 7–Music Day 8–Gym Day 9–Computer	Day 10–Library
2:45 3:00	Pack Up				
3:00 3:30	Dismissal				

Figure 7.10. Kindergarten Schedule

Source: Augusta County Public Schools (2000)

	Monday	Tuesday	Wednesday	Thursday	Friday
8:30 10:00			Reading and Extension		
10:00 10:25	Rug Time/ Calendar	Release Time	Rug Time/ Calendar	Math, Science, Social Studies Language Arts	
10:25 11:00	Printing Journal Word Study	Rug Time/ Calendar	Printing Journal Word Study	Printing Journal Word Study	Printing Journal Word Study
11:00 11:30			Physical Education/ Recess		
11:30 12:20			Math		
12:20 12:45			Lunch		
12:45 1:00			Story		
1:00 1:45			Resource		
1:45 2:30			Unit Work Science, Health, Social Studies		
2:30 2:50			SOL Remediation		
2:50 3:00			Closing/Loading Buses		

Figure 7.11. First Grade Schedule

Source: Augusta County Public Schools (2000)

	Monday	Tuesday	Wednesday	Thursday	Friday
8:30 9:30	Attendance, Lunch Count, Pledge, Calendar, Story Time, Language Arts & Math Problem of the Day, Math, Science & Social Studies Units				
9:30 10:10	Word Study & Language Arts/ Activities				
10:10 11:45	Language Arts Block				
11:45 12:05	Language Arts Activities				
12:05 12:35	Lunch				
12:35 12:55	Language Arts Activities				
12:55 1:40	Special Activities:	Day 1–Guidance Day 2–P.E. Day 3–P.E.	Day 4–Computer Day 5–Music Day 6–Library	Day 7–P.E. Day 8–P.E. Day 9–Computer	Day 10–Music
1:40 2:25	Math Block				Social Studies & Science Units
2:25 2:45	Outside/Inside Physical Education Reward Break Time				
2:30 2:50	SOL Remediation				
2:50 3:00	Closing/Loading Buses				

Figure 7.12. First Grade Schedule

Source: Augusta County Public Schools (2000)

	Monday	Tuesday	Wednesday	Thursday	Friday
8:20 8:35	Opening				
8:35 9:00	Shared Reading Integrated Science/Social Studies				
9:00 10:00	Word Study Groups & Journal				
10:00 11:35	Reading Groups & Extension				
11:35 12:10	Lunch				
12:10 12:35	Recess (Science/Social Studies when have P.E. with Specialist)				
12:35 1:20	Specialists Teacher Planning Time				
1:20 2:20	Math				
2:20 2:40	Science/Social Studies				
2:40 2:50	Story & Snack				
2:50 3:00	Closing/Load Buses				

Figure 7.13.   First Grade Schedule

Source: Augusta County Public Schools (2000)

SUGGESTED KINDERGARTEN SCHEDULE
FOR THE LANGUAGE ARTS BLOCK

8:30 – 8:45	Opening: Collect money, Calendar, Weather, Job Chart
8:45 – 9:00	Show & Tell with sentence dictations recorded
9:00 – 9:15	Big Book Read Aloud/Shared Reading
9:15 – 9:30	Phonemic Awareness Activities
9:30 – 9:50	Journal Writing and Sharing
9:50 – 10:00	Songs/Movement with Phonemic Awareness
10:00 – 10:25	Guided Reading/Phonics Activities w/1st reduced group
10:25 – 10:45	Guided Writing Activities w/ 1st reduced group
10:45 – 11:10	Guided Reading/Phonics Activities w/ 2nd reduced group
11:10 – 11:30	Guided Writing Activities w/ 2nd reduced group

SUGGESTED FIRST GRADE SCHEDULE
FOR THE LANGUAGE ARTS BLOCK

8:30 – 8:45	Opening: Collect money, Calendar, Weather, Job Chart
8:45 – 9:10	Guided Reading/Phonics Activities with 1st reduced group
9:10 – 9:30	Guided Writing Activities w/ 1st reduced group
9:30 – 9:55	Guided Reading/Phonics Activities w/ 2nd reduced group
9:55 – 10:15	Guided Writing Activities w/ 2nd reduced group
10:15 – 10:45	Word Study
10:45 – 11:15	Journal or Writing Workshop
11:15 – 11:30	Read Aloud/Shared Reading

Figure 7.14.
Source: Augusta County Public Schools (2000)

**TIME ALLOTMENTS FOR COMPONENT PARTS OF
READING THEIR WAY**

Kindergarten–First Grade Classroom Teachers

Thirty minutes for phonological awareness (whole group)
Two, forty-minute groups of reduced size:
  • ten minutes for phonics (word study)
  • ten minutes for guided writing
  • twenty minutes for students' guided reading
Forty minutes for writing workshop or journals and sharing
Twenty minutes for shared reading

Kindergarten–First Grade Extension Teachers

Two, forty-five minute sessions of activities to reinforce/enrich classroom instruction, may include: phonological awareness, phonics, reading, and/or writing.

Second Grade–Third Grade Classroom Teachers

Forty minutes for phonics (word study) groups
Two, forty-five minutes for groups of reduced size:
  • twenty-five minutes for students' guided reading
  • ten minutes for word study correlated to reading
  • ten minutes for guided writing as an extension of the reading
Forty minutes for writing workshop or journals and sharing
Ten minutes for shared reading.

Second Grade–Third Grade Extension Teachers

Two, forty-five minute sessions to reinforce/enrich classroom instruction, may include phonics (word study), reading, and/or writing.

Figure 7.15.
Source: Augusta County Public Schools (2000)

As schools have witnessed the benefits of parallel block scheduling, they have extended this approach into second grade. Both of the pilot sites opted to do this during their second year of implementation. We have been successful with this expansion through two very different models.

At one site we created extension centers and time for second grade by scheduling this during the afternoon hours. The second grade teachers conducted their 90-minute whole group instruction during the morning hours but conducted small groups/extension centers after lunch. By scheduling it thusly, the principal was able to utilize the same personnel and space as utilized with the kindergarten and first grade language arts extension centers. This model has worked quite well. Figure 7.16 illustrates this model, as well as depicting the decision to include extension centers for math. This math extension did require additional personnel.

	Monday	Tuesday	Wednesday	Thursday	Friday
8:30 8:40	Administrative Duties, Attendance, Ice Cream, & Lunch Count				
8:40 9:10	Word Study				
9:10 9:40	Physical Education, Art, Handwriting or Remediation				
9:40 10:15	Social Studies & Science				
10:15 11:15	Math & Math Extensions 10:15–10:45 – Session I 10:45–11:15 – Session II				
11:15 12:05	Specials & Planning Time				
12:05 12:35	Lunch & Ice Cream				
12:35 12:45	Remediation				
12:45 1:30	Extension Session I Reading, Writing, & Grammar				
1:30 2:15	Extension Session II Reading, Writing, & Grammar				
2:15 2:50	Today's Language, Today's Math, Remediation, Read Aloud & Closing Activities				
2:50 3:30	Bus Duty & Planning				

Figure 7.16. Second Grade Schedule

Source: Augusta County Public Schools (2000)

At another site we had four sections of second grade. We reassigned one of those second grade teachers as the extension teacher, creating three homerooms. While this did increase the enrollment in the homerooms, these teachers only had one-half of their children for a majority of the day. In this model, all of the children filtered through their extension center for both math and reading/language arts. Thus, we were able to create reduced groups for these two major content areas.

This extension center was equipped with ten computers, a large group gathering area, as well as areas for small group instruction. Figure 7.17 illustrates this model.

Still another option is creating extension areas with learning centers. The children rotate among the various centers, completing the tasks and discussing them with the para-educators. The activities in these learning centers are changed to accommodate learning and concepts.

Schedules may also be developed to combine language arts with social studies instruction in conjunction with extension centers. Math and science instruction may also be developed in conjunction with extension centers. Figures 7.18 and 7.19 illustrate these approaches as suggested by Robert Lynn Canady.

We have found a number of instructional strategies that have proven effective in the extension centers directed by para-educators. They include:

- Poetry folders—collections of poems useful for tracking, reading, and rereading; these poems may or may not be a part of the classroom instruction
- Picture/Word sorts—based on classroom instruction
- Manipulatives—related to phonics and phonological awareness
- Games—related to phonics and phonological awareness
- Computer software—related to skills covered by classroom teacher
- Books—on instructional level for reading by the children

We have also found a lesson design that has proven effective for use in the extension centers directed by a reading specialist. They particularly enjoy the following:

- Rereading familiar material—builds fluency and sight words
- Reading new material—on instructional level

- Writing—creative writing, encouraging invented spellings as well as guided writing, where the children are held accountable for correct spelling
- Comprehension activities—ongoing through various methods (See chapter six for comprehension activities.)

Time	Parakeets & Pelicans	Meadowlarks & Mockingbirds	Flamingos & Flycatchers	Extension
8:15 8:30	Opening Activities (announcements)	Opening Activities (announcements)	Opening Activities (announcements)	Prep for a.m. (announcements)
8:30 9:15	Whole Group Social Studies & Science	Mockingbirds Sm. Grp. Math	Flycatchers Sm. Grp. Math	Meadowlarks & Flamingos Math & Science
9:15 10:00	Parakeets Sm. Grp. Math	Whole Group Social Studies & Science	Flamingos Sm. Grp. Math	Pelicans & Flycatchers Math & Science
10:00 10:45	Pelicans Sm. Grp. Math	Meadowlarks Sm. Grp. Math	Whole Group Social Studies & Science	Parakeets & Mockingbirds Math & Science
10:45 11:30	Library, Music, Guidance or PE	Library, Music, Guidance or PE	Library, Music, Guidance or PE	Planning with 2nd grade teachers
11:30 12:15	Lunch/ Recess	Lunch/ Recess	Lunch/ Recess	Lunch/ Recess
12:15 1:00	Whole Group LA/Word Study	Mockingbirds Sm. Grp. Reading	Flycatchers Sm. Grp. Reading	Meadowlarks & Flamingos LA & SS
1:00 1:45	Parakeets Sm. Grp. Reading	Whole Group LA/Word Study	Flamingos Sm. Grp. Reading	Pelicans & Flycatchers LA & SS
1:45 2:30	Pelicans Sm. Grp. Reading	Meadowlarks Sm. Grp. Reading	Whole Group LA/Word Study	Parakeets & Mockingbirds LA & SS
2:30 2:52	Closing Activities*	Closing Activities*	Closing Activities*	Closing Activities*

Figure 7.17.   Second Grade Schedule

*Closing activities will include SOL remediation, review, and other enrichment activities. Snacks will be eaten during this time period.

Each class will be divided into two groups. While half of the class stays with the homeroom teacher, the other half will go to the extension room.

Other schedules are:
Lunch: 11:30–11:53; 11:34–11:57; 11:38–12:01

Whole group time will be used for Word Study, Daily Oral Language (D.O.L.). Journal/Writing, Science, Social Studies, and Art; all of these activities will be reinforced in the extension room as well.

Source: Augusta County Public Schools (2000)

GRADES 1-3 PARALLEL BLOCK SCHEDULE: OPTION 1-LA/SS & LA EXTENSION					
		Block I 8:20–9:10	**Block II** 9:10–10:00	**Block III** 10:00–10:50	
Teacher A	Homeroom 8:00 – 8:20	LA/SS *RWGs–1,4	RWG–1	RWG–4	
Teacher B		RWG–5	LA/SS RWG–2,5	RWGs–2	
Teacher C		RWG–3	RWG–6	LA/SS RWGs–3,6	
		Language Arts Extension			
Extension		RWGs–2,6	RWGs–3,4	RWGs–1,5	

*RWG = Reading/Writing Group

Figure 7.18. Language Arts, Social Studies Option

Source: Canady, Robert Lynn, "Scheduling Instructional Interventions in Elementary Schools" (2000)

GRADES 1-3 PARALLEL BLOCK SCHEDULE: OPTION 1-MATH/SC & MATH EXTENSION					
		Block IV 11:40–12:30	**Block V** 12:30–1:20	**Block VI** 1:20–2:10	
Teacher A	Lunch and Recess 10:50 – 11:40	Math/SC *MSG–1,4	MSG–1	MSG–4	Planning/Specials 2:10 – 3:00
Teacher B		MSG–5	Math/SC MSGs–2,5	MSG–2	
Teacher C		MSG–3	MSG–6	Math/SC MSGs–3,6	
		Mathematics Extension			
Extension		MSGs–2,6	MSGs–3,4	MSGs–1,5	

*MSG – Math/Science Group

Figure 7.19. Math, Science Option

Source: Canady, Robert Lynn, "Scheduling Instructional Interventions in Elementary Schools" (2000)

Now that teachers have more time and smaller groups with which to work, the discussion turns to what are the most effective and efficient teaching methods. As outlined in previous chapters, it is recommended that kindergarten–first grade teachers concentrate on the following during the course of the day:

- Phonological awareness activities: in small group and whole group
    - Using big books in whole group setting
    - Using picture sorts in whole group setting for review
    - Using object/picture sorts in small group setting for introduction or practice
- Phonics: in small group and whole group
    - Using big books in whole group setting
    - Using word sorts in whole group setting for review
    - Using word sorts in small group setting for introduction
    - Using manipulatives in small group setting for practice
- Contextual reading: in small group and whole group
    - Using read-aloud strategies in whole group
    - Using shared reading strategies in whole group
    - Using guided reading strategies in small group
    - Using choral and echo reading in whole or small group
- Writing: in small group and whole group
    - Using shared writing in whole group
    - Using interactive writing in whole group
    - Using guided writing in small group

Initially, teachers feel that 45-minute reading groups may be too long. They wonder what they will do for 45 minutes. They wonder if the children will be able to attend for that length of time. After just a few days, teachers have found that the 45-minute reading blocks of time are hardly enough time. They realize that certain activities are better suited for use during the 90-minute reading/language arts block and likewise certain activities are better suited for the 45-minute blocks of time.

Following are suggested schedules and activities as found effective by our teachers:

90-Minute Block of Time (whole group instruction):

- Read-Alouds: The whole group setting is wonderful for this experience and the discussion that follows the reading.

- Shared Reading: The whole group setting is perfect for this experience so that the at-risk children may benefit from classmates who are good role models.
- Creative Writing: This activity is typically a bit time consuming, so teachers have found it advantageous to conduct during the longer block of time.
- Word Study: Once the skill has been introduced in small group, practice can occur during the longer block of time. For instance, word study journals, alphabetizing, using words in sentences, drawings to represent the words, buddy sorts are all activities that work well during the 90-minute block of time.
- Concept of Word: This is a wonderful whole group activity when using a big book for demonstration. Using a pocket chart with sentence strips is also effective and efficient for the whole group setting.
- Comprehension: Whole group discussions of stories are a wonderful promoter of comprehension skills.
- Phonological Awareness: All children enjoy the rhyme and rhythm of language. The use of songs, games and stories that support phonological awareness skills is very effective during the whole group setting.

45-Minute Block of Time (small group with classroom teacher):

- Guided Reading: The small group setting provides an excellent time to individualize reading for the child's instructional level. This is the time to listen to each child read and provide support as needed.
- Guided Writing: This block of time is wonderful for those writing assignments where children will be held accountable for their spellings.
- Shared Reading: It is always wonderful to expose books to children and allow them to participate in the reading. This is effective in small group or whole group settings.
- Phonics: Object sorts, picture sorts, and word sorts are appropriate for the small group setting. More individualized attention can be given. This is particularly important if the skill is just being introduced.
- Comprehension: Such activities as writing predictions are appropriate at this time. Comprehension activities directly related to the child's book are desirable.

45-Minute Block (extension center):

• Poetry Folders: A wonderful way to build concept of words, reread material practiced in the classroom and advance vocabulary.
• Journal Writing: A time for creative writing and practice of skills.
• Phonological Awareness: Picture sorts that focus on certain sounds and games/manipulatives that reinforce phonological awareness skills.
• Phonics: Word Sorts and games that focus on letter/sound correspondences.
• Computer Software: To reinforce phonological and phonics skills as introduced by the classroom teacher.
• Comprehension: Activities that relate to the stories and poetry being read in the extension centers.

As outlined in earlier chapters, teachers in grades two through three will not need to spend as much instructional time on phonological awareness. Their reading/language arts blocks of time will be dedicated to reading to the children, children reading, writing and word study. The activities will need to be scheduled into the whole group, small group and extension centers just as the teachers in kindergarten and first grade will do. Children in second and third grades benefit from the small group settings just as the younger children benefit. This type of learning environment accelerates the learning progress of the at-risk population as well as the gifted population, in all grade levels. Cunningham et al.'s work with the Four Blocks (1999) states, "Daily instruction of the components provides numerous and varied opportunities for all children to learn to read and write." This philosophy concurs with the *Reading Their Way* philosophy and components.

The parallel block schedule creates the time. Teachers have to make the decisions of what to do with that time. "Regardless of a school's time schedule, what happens between individual teachers and students in classrooms is still most important, and simply altering the manner in which we schedule schools will not ensure better instruction by teachers or increased learning by students. Consequently, the success or failure of any block schedule will be determined largely by the ability of teachers to harness the potential of the block and improve instruction" (Canady and Rettig, 1996, pg. 27).

Each teacher needs to consider his or her style of teaching and what will work best for them. Some teachers only want to conduct creative writing in small group settings. They feel they can better attend to each child's needs this way. However, because it does usually take a good bit of time, many teachers want to conduct these lessons during the whole group time. It just depends on your preference. Some teachers want to devote the entire 45-minute small group time to reading; others combine this time with reading and word study practice. The important issue is to make sure each child is being read to each day, each child has an opportunity to practice their reading every day, each child has an opportunity for creative writing each day, and every child has an opportunity for word study every day. Strive for the balance!

Expanding and evolving curricula place greater demands on teachers and students every year. Ensuring that students are adequately prepared to meet the challenges of the 21st century demands that we think critically about how we use time in school—that we use it efficiently. As elementary schools build foundations that prepare students for future education, parallel block scheduling resolves concerns about quality instructional time for both teachers and students. Rooted in a foundation of sound educational practice, parallel block scheduling supports the best instructional programs, meeting the needs of students and teachers. Because it is so flexible, it can be adapted to meet specific needs arising from current instructional practices and research. (Hopkins and Canady, 1997, pg. 13.130)

Chapter Eight

Methods of
Reading Instruction

So, the reading groups are established. How will they be instructed? How will the groups be managed? What are the best ways to begin reading a story? What are the best ways to practice reading? How do the teachers keep everyone engaged? Luckily, there are many methods that teachers have found useful.

GUIDED READING

The guided reading strategy is highly recommended. This approach is promoted by Fountas and Pinnell and nicely described in their book, *Guided Reading*. The approach keeps every group member involved in the reading process. The children progress through levels of books according to their reading ability.

In guided reading the lesson begins with an introduction of the book. This is the pre-reading stage of the guided reading lesson. The title is discussed. Children predict what will happen in the book. The teacher may have the children look through the whole book or just portions of the book. As they take this "walk through," the teacher will incorporate any unusual vocabulary into the discussion, thus making future encounters with those words a little easier.

The pre-reading stage of guided reading is most critical. The activities and discussions during this time prepare the children for success in reading. The pre-reading sets the purpose for the reading. If the pre-reading activities are effective, the children will proceed nicely through their reading. We always want to set them up for success.

The next stage of the guided reading approach is the actual reading. The children are responsible for the reading at this time. The teachers are responsible for listening to their reading and supporting them as needed.

Each child has a copy of the text. The children are reading to themselves. Teachers ask the children to read with quiet voices but loud enough for the teacher to be able to hear. This way the teacher can monitor progress. Children raise their hands for assistance if they come to a word that they cannot handle. At this point, the teacher determines what advice to give. Sometimes, the teacher focuses the child's attention on the beginning sound of the word; sometimes there is a small word in the big word; sometimes this word rhymes with a known word; sometimes the picture is a help; and other times the structure of the sentence can help and if the child just rereads, the problem is solved.

The teacher will decide which type of cue to give the children based upon prior instruction and knowledge. Sometimes, it is best to give the semantic cues where the focus is on the meaning of the word. Other times it is more appropriate to give syntactic cues, where the answer is based on the sentence structure. Still other times, it is the visual cues that assist the most, where the relationship between oral language and print is analyzed. Spaces between words and punctuation offer support. The pictures may also offer assistance. Often the teachers will ask, "Does it look right? Does it make sense? Does it sound right?" These questions can jog a child's memory.

Frequently, when teachers ask the children how they figured out a word, the children will give the following explanations:

- I sounded it out.
- I looked at the picture.
- I reread the sentence.

Our goal is to develop independent readers. Teaching them strategies to use on their own is a very worthwhile endeavor. Teaching the children multiple strategies is best.

The last stage in the guided reading approach is the post-reading stage. Here the children are called upon to discuss and analyze the stories. Extensions of stories take place during the post-reading stage. Comprehension is assessed during this portion of the lesson. Often teachers take this opportunity to instruct a spelling lesson directly related to the text. Sometimes it is a review of vocabulary specific to this reading that is discussed. Obviously, a variety of activities may take place during the post-reading time. This is an important stage of reading because it contributes so much to the child's understanding of the text.

The guided reading approach is extremely powerful because it contains the pre-, during, and post-reading stages of the lesson. Every child has an opportunity to read every word of the text. Every child has an opportunity to contribute to discussions and extension activities. This approach endorses and encourages that old adage, "The more you read, the better you read."

CHORAL READING

Another recommended approach to use in reading group is the choral reading method. During choral reading all of the children read the text together. This differs from guided reading in that in choral reading, everyone stays together. They are reading exactly the same words, at the same time, much as in choral singing.

This method is very supportive for children who may be struggling a bit. They hear their neighbor read a word and they can quickly chime in with them. This approach is effective with the nonreaders and beginning readers who are just entering the world of literacy. This approach is not needed once the children begin to read on their own.

Often choral reading takes place with a big book. This is frequently a whole group activity, although it is certainly effective in small group situations as well. The children and the teacher read together.

ECHO READING

Echo reading is an effective method of support reading. During this approach the teacher reads one page and then the child reads that same page, hence the echo effect. The children have the benefit of hearing the text before they are asked to read the text themselves.

Usually echo reading is used with books or charts containing brief text. Ordinarily there is one word, phrase or sentence per page. This is an approach most appropriate for nonreaders or children just entering the world of reading. This approach is not necessary for those students who are already reading on their own. Echo reading is for children who need repetition of the text.

BUDDY READING

Buddy reading is a wonderful approach to use with children who have begun to read. It is appropriate with early readers as well as more accomplished readers. During buddy reading, two children are paired and they take turns reading the story to each other.

The teacher usually selects the students who will be buddies for reading. In some cases, the teacher may select students because they are of similar ability. Other times, the teacher may place a weaker student with a higher-ability student. Selection would depend on the purpose of the reading.

Buddy reading can be organized in a variety of ways. For example, one child could read the entire book to the other child, who is listening and assisting if needed. Upon completion, the roles would switch and the other child would be the reader. In this scenario, children of similar or differing abilities could be grouped together.

Sometimes, buddy reading is arranged so that one child reads one page and the other child reads the next page. The readers continue to take turns until the book is completed. During reading the children help one another as needed. Generally, these buddies would be on the same reading level.

Still another method of buddy reading is arranged around the characters of the story. Each reader is assigned the parts of characters and they read only when those characters are speaking. One reader is usually assigned the narrator portions as well. This method would be for children reading at higher levels as they would be able to adjust to this arrangement more easily.

Practice is the main purpose with any model of buddy reading. Again, we think of the old adage, "The more you read, the better you read." Buddy reading is a way to reread and still keep it interesting for the children. Generally speaking, children enjoy reading with a friend. Often they are allowed to sit on the floor or in very relaxed, comfortable places for this type of reading. The teacher rotates among the children to monitor progress and time on task.

INDIVIDUAL READING

During the reading group, you may want to have individual children read orally. This is certainly one method for ascertaining the reading proficiency of the students. It is usually best to allow the children to look over the text before they are asked to read aloud. This quick peek helps to prepare the children for success.

Individual reading time is the perfect time for taking running records. Running records are a form of assessment where the teacher records the child's reading errors. This assessment can help the teacher determine the reading level of the student. The teacher may choose to share the assessment results with the student or may retain the running record for documentation and discussion at a later date.

Running records should be an ongoing form of assessment in every classroom. Teachers may choose to conduct a running record on one child from each group, each day. Sometimes teachers prefer to conduct running records on everyone in the reading group, perhaps once a month.

Reading specialists also conduct running records. It is helpful for classroom teachers and reading specialists to compare results and make judgments of reading placement.

Round robin individual reading is not recommended. This is the method where children are directed to read according to their seating order. For example, the teacher starts to her right and circulates around the table from one child to the next, to the next, etc. In this model, children often are not attentive unless it is their turn to read. They often count ahead to their page and try to get ready. While round robin is managed easily, other methods are much more effective and efficient.

TIMED/REPEATED READINGS

Reading fluency is one major goal of all classroom teachers. Practice helps. Rereading can be boring for children if always conducted in the same manner. Timed/repeated readings are another way to practice that is usually fun and beneficial for children.

A stopwatch is needed for this method. The teacher can time the children or older children can be taught this process. Timed/repeated readings are generally conducted about once or twice a month.

With this method, the initial reading of text is timed. That time is recorded and the child tries to beat that time on subsequent readings. If an error is made in reading, the child must correct that error while the timer is still running. After each reading the time is recorded and progress evaluated. The purpose is to build fluency along with accurate reading.

Many teachers use this approach in conjunction with small group reading. Children may be sent to another part of the room or into the hallway to conduct this activity. At other times, the teacher will time one child from each group at the reading table. Sometimes, this activity is conducted at another time during the day. Valuable instructional information is gained through this technique.

SILENT SUSTAINED READING

Reading practice is also attained through periods of silent sustained reading. Usually this lasts for approximately twenty minutes. It is most beneficial if it occurs daily.

During silent sustained reading, children are reading on their instructional or independent level. They are reading to themselves. Usually the material is self-selected by the student. The teacher will monitor to ensure material of the proper level has been selected.

Children often lay on the floor or are seated in comfortable areas for this portion of the reading time. Again this creates an opportunity for re-reading and practice. Timed/repeated readings could be conducted at this time, particularly if children are able to time themselves.

Younger children may need to select several books for this activity or they may need to be allowed to exchange a book when they have finished it. This is because their books are usually shorter. Children of higher reading ability, however, should be asked to keep the one book they selected. This will lessen the movement and disruptions in the classroom.

There is no one certain way to conduct reading groups. All of the above mentioned methods are appropriate and effective. Variety is the spice of life—keep reading fun and exciting. Keep your purpose in the forefront and select the method that best suits that purpose. Happy reading!

Chapter Nine

Assessment and Evaluation

Believing in Children Is Paramount
High Expectations Are Crucial
Teaching on Their Instructional Level Is Mandatory

This is the philosophy statement of *Reading Their Way*. Assessments and evaluation tools must be in place in order to fulfill this philosophy. These assessments and evaluations should be ongoing throughout the school year.

Nothing is better than an observant teacher. Daily kid-watching is one of the best assessment/evaluation tools available. The needs of children are constantly changing as they are learning. Because of this, teachers need to be constantly keeping pace with the instructional needs of their students. Daily observations can make this happen. These observations should be made during oral or silent reading, comprehension tasks, phonics activities, phonological awareness lessons and writing.

Along with daily observations, teachers should utilize informal assessments. These may be teacher-made or commercially rendered. Again, these assessments should be ongoing and cover all areas of reading/language arts instruction. One type of useful informal assessment would be a rubric. Many writing rubrics are available on the market for teacher use. Informal reading inventories are also readily available. Spelling inventories are accessible.

The use of running records is highly recommended for determining the reading level of children. Running records also provide information pertaining to the types of errors children make in oral reading. Error analysis is very informative for instruction. *An Observation Survey of Early Literacy*

Achievement by Marie M. Clay (1994) is an excellent resource on administering running records. *Guided Reading* by Irene C. Fountas and Gay Su Pinnell (1996) is also an excellent resource on the use of running records.

Assessments and evaluations of progress should occur at least three times a year; fall, winter and spring are recommended. It is beneficial to collect such data within grade levels and across grade levels so that growth comparisons may be made as the children proceed through the grades.

The PALS (Phonological Awareness Literacy Screening) assessment, developed by personnel at the University of Virginia, has proven to be very beneficial. This assessment is relatively easy to administer. The results provide wonderful information upon which to base instruction. This assessment may be purchased from the University of Virginia Bookstore, Charlottesville, Virginia [http://curry.edschool.virginia.edu/centers/pals].

At the kindergarten level, PALS assesses rhyming, beginning sounds, letter sound recognition, lower case letter recognition, spelling and word recognition in isolation. At the first through third grade levels, PALS consists of a spelling inventory, informal reading inventory and phonological awareness inventory (if necessary). Teachers readily learn the reading level of students as well as areas of strength or weakness.

It is recommended that the PALS or a similar assessment be administered twice a year: fall and spring. This time line will allow the teachers to gauge student progress and also provides for the collection of wonderful documentation to use in parent conferences.

Setting benchmarks is a helpful tool for evaluating student progress as well as the effectiveness of your program. In *Reading Their Way* we have the following benchmarks:

By the end of kindergarten—finish the first preprimer level reader
By the end of first grade—finish the 1.2 level reader
By the end of second grade—finish the 2.2 level reader
Meeting these benchmarks will ensure that our children are entering third
    grade, reading at the third grade level.
By the end of third grade—finish the 3.2 level reader

In actuality, the *Reading Their Way* children are surpassing these benchmarks. Some kindergarten children leave kindergarten reading at the 1.1

level. Many first grade children leave that grade level reading at the 2.2 level, and so on. It is important that assessments be in place at the beginning of each year to ascertain the current reading level. Continuous progress is important. Once teachers determine the instructional reading level, lessons should begin at that level and allow children to progress at their own speed. Allow them to progress and enjoy books at their rate. Teachers at all grade levels should be trained and have materials to offer excellent instruction to children at various reading levels, at any grade level. Do not put limits on children.

Appendix A

Sequence of Sounds and Activities

GRADES K–3

Instruction should always be based on the needs of the students. Assessments help to determine a child's instructional level; however, teachers need to be constant "kid-watchers" and adjust lessons appropriately.

The sequences presented here are designed for the majority of the students on that grade level although some students may require more review of skills presented at previous levels. Some students may be functioning above grade level and need to begin "midway" through the sequence and progress into the design for the next grade level.

The intention is that each step of the sequence be taught for three to five days. In reality, some children only require two days of instruction per step. Some children require the full five days. Teachers should always pace instruction according to individual needs.

Kindergarten

1. Introduce the sounds /m/ and /t/ with 3-dimensional letters
   a. Use the introductory method discussed in chapter three
   b. Pace according to individal needs
2. Introduce the sounds /p/ and /r/ with 3-dimensional letters
   a. Use the introductory method discussed in chapter three
   b. Pace according to individual needs
3. Contrast all four sounds with the 3-dimensional letters
   a. Supplement with object sorts
   b. Supplement with picture sorts

4. Write the four sounds
   a. Teacher says sounds and child write them
   b. Use object and picture sorts, asking child to write beginning sounds
5. Teach short vowel sound /a/ and consonant /s/
   a. Use the introductory method discussed in chapter three
   b. Pace according to individual needs
6. Compare and contrast all six sounds
   a. Use three sorts at a time
   b. Use objects and pictures
7. Make words with the /at/ word family. Use: rat, sat, pat, mat, cat
   a. Display the word family using the 3-dimensional letters
   b. Display the picture or object for the word
   c. Place the sounds from beginning to end of word, blending as you go
   d. Slide your finger along and read the completed word
8. Other "making word" strategies
   a. Read spelled word with picture support
   b. Read spelled word without picture support
   c. Read flash cards of spelled words
   d. Write words as teacher says them
   e. Read lists of rhyming words
   f. Read flip books of rhyming words
9. Make words with the /ap/ word family. Use: tap, map, rap, sap
   a. Use same procedure as /at/ word family
   b. Compare and contrast /at/ and /ap/ words
   c. Make words with the /am/ family. Use: ram, Pam, Sam, ham
   d. Compare and contrast with /at/ and /ap/ words
10. Continue to introduce two sounds at a time
    a. Compare and contrast with mastered sounds
    b. Make words with a variety of word families—not all of them
    c. Suggested sequence of sounds:
       c, n
       b, o
       ot family–pot, cot, dot, rot
       op family–mop, top, pop, cop
       ob family–cob, sob, mob, rob
       l, f

h, d

g, i

it family–sit, fit, hit, lit

ig family–fig, big, pig, dig

id family–lid, hid, did, rid

k, v

j, u

ug family–jug, mug, rug, bug

ut family–cut, hut, nut, gut

up family–cup, pup, up

z, y

e, w

et family–wet, pet, let, met

eg family–peg, beg, leg, Meg

ed family–Ted, red, bed, fed

q, x

ch, th

sh, wh

11. Teach sight words
    a. Should have a concept of word
    b. Should be comfortable making words using 3-dimensional letters
    c. Introduce with flash cards: the a is on
    d. Note sight words on charts and in books
    e. May introduce after the "at" family; as occur in books
12. Writing
    a. Make sentences using mastered phonetic spellings
    b. Make sentences using sight words
    c. Write something every day
    d. Hold children accountable for phonetic spellings/sight words
    e. Allow inventive spelling in journals and projects
13. Books
    a. Introduce decodable books, if you haven't already
    b. Continue reading to the children from a variety of literature
14. Reading Group Strategies
    a. Teacher introduces book by discussing title and predicting
    b. Teacher incorporates unusual vocabulary into introduction
    c. Choral Reading

    d. Echo Reading
    e. Individuals Read (not Round Robin)
    f. Guided Reading
    g. Buddy Reading
    h. Timed-Repeated Readings

First Grade

1. Review /ă/ *vs* /ĭ/
    a. Use manipulative letters
    b. Use object/picture sorts
    c. Word sorts CvC words: /at/ *vs* /it/; /ap/ *vs* /ip/
    d. Write CvC words using the above families
    e. Read CvC words in lists and in books
2. Review /ŏ/ *vs* /ŭ/
    a. Use manipulative letters
    b. Use object/picture sorts
    c. Word sort CvC words with: /ot/ *vs* /ut/; /og/ *vs* /ug/
    d. Write CvC words using the above families
    e. Read CvC words in lists and in books
3. Compare and contrast /ă/, /ŏ/, /ĭ/, /ŭ/
    a. Use manipulative letters
    b. Use object/picture sorts
    c. Word sort with the four sounds; vary ending sounds
    d. Write words with the four sounds; vary word families
    e. Read books with these sounds
4. Review /ŭ/ *vs* /ĕ/
    a. Use manipulative letters
    b. Use object/picture sorts
    c. Word sort CvC words with: /ut/ *vs* /et/; /ug/ *vs* /eg/
    d. Write CvC words using the above families
    e. Read CvC words in lists and in books
5. Review /ch/ *vs* /th/
    a. Use object/picture sorts
    b. Word sort /ch/ *vs* /th/
    c. Write words using /ch/ and /th/
    d. Read lists of words and books containing these sounds

Proceed with the following sequence, using the same step as #5:

6. Review /sh/ *vs* /wh/
7. Compare and contrast /ch/, /th/, /sh/, /wh/
8. Introduce /b/ *vs* /bl/
9. Introduce /c/ *vs* /cl/
10. Introduce /s/ *vs* /sl/
11. Introduce /f/ *vs* /fl/
12. Introduce /g/ *vs* /gl/
13. Introduce /p/ *vs* /pl/
14. Compare and contrast /bl/, /cl/, /sl/, /fl/, /gl/, /pl/
15. Introduce /s/ *vs* /sp/
16. Introduce /s/ *vs* /sn/
17. Introduce /s/ *vs* /st/
18. Introduce /s/ *vs* /sm/
19. Compare and contrast /sp/, /sn/, /st/, /sm/
20. Introduce /st/ *vs* /str/
21. Introduce /d/ *vs* /dr/
22. Introduce /g/ *vs* /gr/
23. Introduce /p/ *vs* /pr/
24. Introduce /t/ *vs* /tr/
25. Compare and contrast /str/, /dr/, /gr/, /pr/, /tr/
    a. Compare and contrast three at a time

Introduce the long vowel pattern (vCe) by contrasting with short vowels using: picture sorts, object sorts, and then word sorts, reading lists, books, and writing. Use the following sequence, pacing according to the needs of the children:

26. /ă/ *vs* /a_e/
27. /ŏ/ *vs* /o_e/
28. Compare and contrast /a_e/ *vs* /o_e/
29. /ĭ/ *vs* /i_e/
30. /ŭ/ *vs* /u_e/
31. Compare and contrast /i_e/ *vs* /u_e/
32. /ĕ/ *vs* /ee/
33. Compare and contrast all five patterns, three at a time

34. Introduce /ank/ *vs* /ink/
    a. Use object/picture sorts
    b. Word sort /ank/ *vs* /ink/
    c. Write words using /ank/ and /ink/
    d. Read lists of words and books containing these sounds

Proceed with the following sequence, using the same steps as #34:

35. Compare and contrast /ank/ *vs* /unk/
36. Compare and contrast /ank/ *vs* /unk/ *vs* /ink/
37. Introduce /ang/ *vs* /ing/
38. Compare and contrast /ing/ *vs* /ung/
39. Compare and contrast /ing/ *vs* /ung/ *vs* /ang/

Introduce the following long vowel patterns by contrasting with short vowels and the vCe patterns. Use picture sorts, object sorts, word sorts, reading books, and writing. Use the following sequence, pacing according to the needs of the children:

40. /ă/ *vs* /ai/
41. /ai/ *vs* /ay/
42. /a_e/ *vs* /ai/ and /ay/
43. /ŏ/ *vs* /oa/
44. /o_e/ *vs* /oa/ *vs* /o/ (as in "so")
45. Compare and contrast /ai/, /ay/ *vs* /oa/, /o/
46. /ĭ/ *vs* /i_e/
47. /ĭ/ *vs* /y/
48. /y/ *vs* /i_e/
49. /ŭ/ *vs* /u_e/
50. /ĕ/ *vs* /ea/
51. /ee/ and /ea/ *vs* /e/ (as in "me")
52. Compare and contrast various vowels, three at a time
53. Introduce /_sk/ *vs* /_sh/
    a. Use object/picture sorts
    b. Word sort /_sk/ and /_sh/
    c. Write words using /_sk/ and /_sh/
    d. Read lists of words and books containing these sounds

Proceed with the following sequence, using the same steps as #53:

54. Introduce /_mp/ *vs* /_nd/
55. Compare and contrast /_sk/, /_sh/, /_mp/, /_nd/
56. Introduce /ack *vs* /ock/
57. Introduce /ick/ *vs* /uck/
58. Compare and contrast /ack/, /ock/, /ick/, /uck/
59. Introduce /ast/ *vs* /ist/
60. Introduce /est/ *vs* /ust/
61. Compare and contrast /ast/, /ist/, /est/, /ust/
62. Introduce /all/ *vs* /ell/
63. Compare /all/, /ell/, /ast/, /est/

Second Grade

1. Review /ank/ *vs* /ink/
   a. Use object picture sorts
   b. Word sort /ank/ *vs* /ink/
   c. Write words using /ank/ and /ink/
   d. Read lists of words and books containing these sounds
2. Review /ing/ *vs* /ong/
   a. Use object picture sorts
   b. Word sort /ing/ *vs* /ong/
   c. Write words using /ing/ and /ong/
   d. Read list of words and books containing these sounds
3. Review /all/ *vs* /ell/
   a. Use object picture sorts
   b. Word sort /all/ *vs* /ell/
   c. Write words using /all/ and /ell/
   d. Read lists of words and books containing these sounds
4. Compare and contrast the above vowel patterns, three at a time
5. Review /ast/ *vs* /ist/
   a. Use object/picture sorts
   b. Word sort /ast/ *vs* /ist/
   c. Write words using /ast/ and /ist/
   d. Read lists of words and books containing these sounds

6. Review /ust/ *vs* /est/
   a. Use object/picture sorts
   b. Word sort /ust/ *vs* /est/
   c. Write words using /ust/ and /est/
   d. Read list of words and books containing these sounds
7. Compare and contrast /ast/ *vs* /ist/ *vs* /ust/ *vs* /est/
   a. Use object/picture sorts
   b. Word sort /ast/ *vs* /ist/ *vs* /ust/ vs /est/
   c. Write words using these patterns
   d. Read lists of words and books containing these sounds

Review long vowel patterns with the following activities and sequences:

Picture Sorts
Word Sorts
Object Sorts
Dictated Lists
Creative Writing
Poems
Books

  8. Review /ă/ *vs* /a_e/
  9. Review /a_e/ *vs* /ay/
10. Review /ai/ *vs* /ay/
11. Review /a_e/ *vs* /ai/ *vs* /ay/
12. Introduce /ar/ *vs* /a_e/
13. Review /ĭ/ *vs* /i_e/
14. Review /i_e/ *vs* /y/
15. Introduce /i_e/ *vs* /igh/
16. Introduce /i_e/ *vs* /ir/
17. Compare and contrast /ar/ *vs* /ir/
18. Compare and contrast /i_e/ *vs* /y/ *vs* /igh/
19. Review /ŏ/ *vs* /o_e/
20. Review /ŏ/ *vs* /oa/
21. Introduce /oa/ *vs* /or/
22. Introduce /ol/ *vs* /ow/ (i.e. "told, sold, bolt" *vs* "tow, sow, bow")
23. Compare and contrast /o_e/ *vs* /oa/ *vs* /or/
24. Compare and contrast /or/ *vs* /ol/ *vs* /ow/

25. Review /ŭ/ *vs* /u_e/
26. Introduce /u_e/ *vs* /ue/
27. Introduce /u_e/ *vs* /ur/
28. Compare and contrast /ue/ *vs* /ur/
29. Introduce /ur/ *vs* /ui/
30. Compare and contrast /u/ *vs* /ur/ *vs* /ui/
31. Review /ĕ/ *vs* /ee/
32. Review /ĕ/ *vs* /ea/
33. Introduce /ee/ *vs* /er/
34. Introduce /ea/ *vs* /ie/ (e.g. cheat *vs* chief; neat *vs* niece)
35. Compare and contrast /er/ *vs* /ie/
36. Review /ar/ *vs* /ir/
37. Review /or/ *vs* /ur/
38. Review /ar/ *vs* /er/
39. Compare and contrast /ar/, /er/, /ir/, /ur/
40. Compare and contrast /or/, /er/, /ir/, /ur/

Introduce the following patterns with the indicated activities and sequence:

Picture Sorts	Dictated Lists
Words Sorts	Contextual Reading
Word Games	Creative Writing

41. Introduce /qu/ and /squ/
42. Introduce /scr/ *vs* /shr/
43. Compare and contrast /qu/, /squ/, /scr/, /shr/
44. Introduce /spl/ *vs* /spr/
45. Introduce /str/ *vs* /thr/
46. Compare and contrast /spl/, /spr/, /str/, /thr/
47. Introduce /_ck/ *vs* /_ke/
48. Introduce /_ch/ *vs* /_tch/
49. Compare and contrast /_ck/, /_ke/, /_ch/, /_tch/
50. Introduce /ew/ *vs* /oo/
51. Introduce /oy/ *vs* /oi/
52. Compare and contrast /ew/ *vs* /oy/
53. Compare and contrast /oo/ *vs* /oi/
54. Introduce /ou/ *vs* /ow/

55. Compare and contrast /oy/, /oi/, /ou/, /ow/
56. Introduce /au/ *vs* /aw/
57. Introduce /ew/ *vs* /aw/
58. Compare and contrast /au/ *vs* /ew/
59. Introduce /au/ *vs* /al/
60. Compare and contrast /ew/, /au/, /al/, /aw/

Introduce and review the following word groups with the suggested activities:

Picture Sorts	Contextual Reading
Word Sorts	Dictated Lists
Word Games	Creative Writing

61. Homophones
62. Contractions

Third Grade

1. Review /ă/ *vs* /a_e/ *vs* /ay/
2. Review /ai/ *vs* /ar/
3. Review /ĭ/ *vs* /i_e
4. Review /i_e/ *vs* /ir/
5. Review /ŏ/ *vs* /oa/
6. Review /oa/ *vs* /or/
7. Review /ŭ/ *vs* /u_e/
8. Review /u_e/ *vs* /ur/
9. Review /ĕ/ *vs* /ee/
10. Review /ee/ *vs* /er/
11. Review /ar/ *vs* /ir/ *vs* /or/
12. Review /ur/ *vs* /er/ *vs* /ar/
13. Review /ew/ *vs* /oo/
14. Review /oy/ *vs* /oi/
15. Review /ou/ *vs* /ow/
16. Compare and contrast /oo/ *vs* /oi/ *vs* /ou/
17. Review /au/ *vs* /aw/
18. Review /au/ *vs* /al/
19. Compare and contrast /au/ *vs* /aw/ *vs* /al

20. Compare and contrast "ed" sounds
    (/ĭd/ = acted *vs* /d/ = aimed *vs* /t/ = asked)
21. Review homophones
22. Review contractions
23. Introduce compound words
24. Introduce "ed" and "ing" with no change to base word
    (ask: asked, asking; aim: aimed, aiming)
25. Introduce "ed" and "ing" with doubling; bat (batted, batting)
26. Introduce "ed" and "ing" with e-drop (no doubling)
    (bake: baked, baking)
27. Compare and contrast #25 and #26
    (hop: hopped, hopping / hope: hoped, hoping)
28. Compare and contrast /sc/, /scr/, /spl/
29. Compare and contrast /sh/, /shr/, /_sh/
30. Compare and contrast /st/, /str/, /_st/
31. Compare and contrast /k/, /ck/, /ke/
32. Compare and contrast /ch/, /_ch/, /_tch/
33. Compare and contrast /_dge/, /_ge/
34. Compare and contrast soft /g/ and hard /g/ (gel *vs* gift)
35. Compare and contrast /kn/ and /gn/ (knock and gnarl
36. Compare and contrast /mb/ and /wr/ (comb and wrap)

Suggested Resources

Magnetic Dry-Erase boards
Dry-Erase markers
Magnetic letters—vowels one color, consonants another color
Beginning sound object sorts
Picture sorts
Word sorts
Decodable books
Predictable, repetitive books
Nonfiction books
Good literature
Variety of writing utensils
Variety of manipulatives (puppets, educational games, etc.)
Resources of phonemic awareness activities:
  Phonemic Awareness, Fitzpatrick
  Take Home Phonological Awareness, Robertson and Salter
  Phonemic Awareness in Young Children, Adams, Foorman, Lundberg
    and Beeler
Resources on leveling readers:
  Guided Reading, Fountas and Pinnell
  Matching Books to Readers, Fountas and Pinnell
Leveling guides of publishing companies

References

Adams, M.J. (1990). *Beginning to Read: Thinking and Learning about Print.* Cambridge, MA: MIT Press.

Adams, M.J., Foorman, B.R., Lundberg, I., & Beeler, T. (1998). *Phonemic Awareness in Young Children.* Baltimore, MD.: Brookes.

Bear, D.R., Invernizzi, M., Templeton, S., & Johnston, F. (1996). *Words Their Way.* Edgewood Cliffs, NJ: Prentice-Hall.

Blachman, B. (1991). *Getting Ready to Read.* Timonium, MD: York Press, Inc.

Burns, M., Griffin, P., & Snow, C. (1999). *Starting Out Right.* Washington, DC: National Academy Press.

Canady, R.L. (1990). Parallel Block Scheduling: A Better Way to Organize a School. *Principal,* January, 34–36.

Canady, R.L. (2000). Scheduling Instructional Interventions in Elementary School (presented at the Making Instructional Time Count Conference; Charlottesville, VA).

Canady, R. & Rettig, M. (1996). *Teaching in the Block: Strategies for Engaging Active Learners.* Larchmont, NY: Eye on Education.

Clay, M.M. (1985). *The Early Detection of Reading Difficulties* (3rd ed.). Portsmouth, NH: Heinemann.

Clay, M.M. (1994). *An Observation Survey of Early Literacy Achievement.* Auckland, NZ: Heinemann.

Cunningham, A.E. (1990). Explicit versus Implicit Instruction in Phonemic Awareness. *Journal of Experimental Child Psychology,* 50: 429–444.

Cunningham, P., Hall, D., & Sigmon, C. (1999). *The Teacher's Guide to the Four Blocks.* Greensboro, NC: Carson-Dellosa.

Fielding-Barnesley, R. (1997). Explicit Instruction in Decoding Benefits Children High in Phonemic Awareness and Alphabet Knowledge. *Scientific Studies of Reading,* 1(1): 85–98.

Fitzpatrick, J. (1997). *Phonemic Awareness.* Cypress, CA: Creative Teaching Press.

Fountas, I.C. & Pinnell, G.S. (1996). *Guided Reading.* Portsmouth, NH: Heinemann.

Fountas, I.C. & Pinnell, G.S. (1999). *Matching Books to Readers.* Portsmouth, NH: Heinemann.

Ganske, K. (2000). *Word Journeys.* New York, NY: Guilford.

Griffith, P.L. & Klesius, J.P. (1990). The Effect of Phonemic Awareness Ability and Reading Instructional Approach on First Grade. Paper presented at the National Reading Conference (40th; Miami, FL, Nov. 27–Dec. 1, 1990). ED332160

Griffith, P. & Olson, M. (1992). Phonemic Awareness Helps Beginning Readers Break the Code. *The Reading Teacher,* vol. 45, no. 7, March.

Harvey, S. & Goudvis, A. (2000). *Strategies That Work.* York, ME: Stenhouse.

Hopkins, H. & Canady, R.L. (1997). Parallel Block Scheduling for Elementary Schools, *Association for Supervision and Curriculum Development,* 13.109–13.131.

International Reading Association. (2000). Teaching All Children to Read: The Roles of the Reading Specialist. *The Reading Teacher,* vol. 54, no. 1, September.

Invernizzi, M., Meier, J., Swank, L., Juel, C. & The Virginia State Department of Education. (2000). *Phonological Awareness Literacy Screening [PALS] Teachers Manual.* Charlottesville: The University of Virginia at the Curry School of Education.

Juel, C. (1988). Learning to Read and Write: A Longitudinal Study of 54 Children from First through Fourth Grades. *Journal of Educational Psychology,* 80(4): 437–447.

Lundberg, I., Frost, J., & Peterson, D.P. (1988). Effects of an Extensive Program for Stimulating Phonological Awareness in Preschool Children. *Reading Research Quarterly,* 23, 264–284.

Lyon, G.R. (1996). Why Johnny Can't Decode. *Washington Post Education Review.* October 27.

National Education Commission on Time and Learning. (1994). *Prisoners of Time: Report of the National Education Commission on Time and Learning.* Washington, DC: U.S. Government Printing Office.

Robertson, C. & Salter, W. (1998). *Take Home Phonological Awareness.* East Moline, IL: LinguiSystems.

Snow, C., Burns, M., & Griffin, P. (1998). *Preventing Reading Difficulties in Young Children.* Washington, DC: National Academy Press.

Wasserstein, P. (2000/2001). Putting Readers in the Driver's Seat. *Education Leadership,* December/January: 74–77.

About the Author

Dorothy J. Donat is an elementary curriculum supervisor in a public school system. She works primarily with pre-kindergarten through third grade teachers, where early intervention is stressed. Dorothy also works with Title I teachers on improving language arts skills for students in kindergarten through third grades.

Dorothy trains her division's classroom teachers, administrators, Title I teachers, special education teachers, and para-educators in using the *Reading Their Way* approach. She has also conducted training sessions in Kentucky, Texas, Virgin Islands, and many school divisions in Virginia. These training sessions are followed by ongoing classroom observations, teacher conferences, share fairs, and make-it/take-it workshops. Dorothy is committed to teaching children to read and believes one way to ensure this is through teacher training.

Dorothy lives in the Shenandoah Valley of Virginia with her husband and two children. She enjoys hiking, jogging and reading.